# THE BYZANTINE WORLD WAR

# THE BYZANTINE
# WORLD WAR

*The Last Romans
and the First Crusaders*

NICK HOLMES

Matador
9 Priory Business Park,
Wistow Road, Kibworth Beauchamp,
Leicestershire. LE8 0RX
Tel: 0116 279 2299
Email: books@troubador.co.uk
Web: www.troubador.co.uk/matador
Twitter: @matadorbooks

ISBN 978 1789017 588

British Library Cataloguing in Publication Data.
A catalogue record for this book is available from the British Library.

Printed and bound in the UK by T J International, Padstow, Cornwall
Typeset in 11pt Adobe Jenson Pro by Troubador Publishing Ltd, Leicester, UK

Matador is an imprint of Troubador Publishing Ltd

*In memory of my parents,*
*for their kindness, patience and wisdom.*

# Contents

## Part I
### The Forgotten Empire

## Part II
### The Battle for Byzantium

## Part III
### The First Crusaders

# LIST OF MAPS

# Cast of Characters

## *The Byzantines*

Basil II — Emperor, 976–1025: nicknamed the Bulgar-Slayer

Katakolon Kekaumenos — General who successfully defended Armenia against the Seljuk Turks in the 1040s and 1050s

Constantine X Doukas — Emperor, 1059–67, in whose reign the Turks conquered Byzantine Armenia and began raiding Anatolia

Eudocia Makrembolitissa — Empress, first married to Constantine X and then Romanus Diogenes

Romanus IV Diogenes — Emperor, 1068–71, who fought and lost the Battle of Manzikert

Michael VII Doukas — Emperor, 1071–78. Constantine X's eldest son and co-Emperor with Romanus Diogenes before claiming

|  | the throne himself in 1071 in a palace coup |
| --- | --- |
| Caesar John Doukas | Brother of Constantine X and regent to his children after Constantine's death |
| Andronicus Doukas | Son of Caesar John, commander of rear-guard at Manzikert |
| Michael Attaleiates | Senator, lawyer and author of the main history of Romanus Diogenes' reign |
| Michael Psellus | Senator, lawyer, philosopher and author of several books on history, law and philosophy |
| Theodore Alyates | Cappadocian general, loyal supporter of Romanus Diogenes and commander of the right wing at Manzikert |
| Nicephorus Bryennius | Commander of the western army and led the left wing at Manzikert |
| Constantine Doukas | Other son of Caesar John |
| Nicephorus III Botaneiates | Emperor, 1078–81, he usurped the throne from Michael VII Doukas |
| Alexius I Comnenus | Emperor, 1081–1118, and founder of the Comnenian dynasty |

## THE TURKS AND ARABS

Tughril           Great Seljuk Sultan, 1038–63, co-ruled with Chaghri in the East and occupied Baghdad in 1055

Alp Arslan           Great Seljuk Sultan, 1063–72, fought at the Battle of Manzikert

Malik-Shah           Great Seljuk Sultan, 1072–92

Afsin           Renegade Turkish warlord who sacked several Byzantine cities in 1067–9

Kilij Arslan           Seljuk Sultan of the Anatolia region (called Rum)

Duqaq of Damascus           Seljuk ruler of Damascus at time of First Crusade

Ridwan of Aleppo           Seljuk ruler of Aleppo at time of First Crusade

Kerbogha           Ruler of Mosul and leader of Muslim army to relieve Antioch from the First Crusade

Al-Afdal           Fatimid ruler of Egypt at time of First Crusade

# THE CRUSADERS

Pope Urban II
Launched the First Crusade at Clermont in 1095

Bohemond of Taranto
Son of Robert Guiscard and leader of the southern Italian Norman crusaders

Godfrey of Bouillon
Duke of Lower Lotharingia and leader of crusaders from Lotharingia and Germany

Raymond of Toulouse
Leader of the southern French crusaders

Robert of Flanders
Leading figure among the northern French crusaders

Peter the Hermit
Preacher and leader of the People's Crusade

Stephen of Blois
Count of Blois and leading figure among the northern French crusaders

Peter Bartholomew
Peasant visionary in whose dream Christ purportedly showed him the location of the Holy Lance

# Note on Proper Names

In the interests of accessibility, I have used familiar Latinate forms of proper names for the more famous characters rather than their Greek, Turkish or Arab originals. For example, Romanus Diogenes is used rather than Romanos Diogenes, as it would be in Greek. However, for less well-known figures, I have used the original spelling or as close to it as I can achieve.

# INTRODUCTION

With smoke billowing around him, Ludolf of Tournai felt he could almost touch the walls of Jerusalem.

But they stood beyond his reach – a vision of brilliant white stone in front of his siege tower. He knew that if he raised his head above the parapet, a swarm of iron arrowheads would shatter his skull. The city had been in Arab hands for over 400 years. No Christian army had come close to it for centuries. Now these men, the first crusaders, were at their last gasp. Reduced to some 14,000 from over 100,000 that had marched east, they barely had the strength to mount this last desperate attempt to capture the holy city.

To the south, the crusaders' only other siege tower attracted a hail of Arab incendiary missiles. Riddled with burning pitch shot by catapults, the tower was a smoking wreck. The soldiers inside stumbled out, dazed and despairing. It seemed as if God had abandoned them in their final hour.

Now it was up to Ludolf. Little did he know it, but in a few minutes he would become one of the heroes of the Middle Ages. That morning, he and his men had managed to push their siege tower right up to the walls, miraculously surviving the missiles from the Arab catapults. Now they were too close for the catapults to strike them. For the last hour, they had exchanged shots with the defenders: arrows, crossbow bolts, rocks, whatever each side could get their hands on.

Suddenly, the enemy barrage stopped. Ludolf counted to twelve. Still no sound. Curiosity overcame him. He dared to peer over the parapet. To his relief, no arrows came. Instead, he could see that a part of the walls beneath them was on fire. Thick black smoke enveloped the battlements. Something was wrong.

Ludolf acted on instinct. He seized one of the planks of hide-covered wattle that the crusaders had been crouching behind and threw it down as a makeshift bridge between the siege tower and the wall. His heart pounding and half expecting to die, he turned to his men and shouted the battle cry: "Deus vult" – God wills it! Then, sword in hand, he charged across the chasm.

There were no defenders to meet him. Choking from the smoke and scarcely believing his luck, he jumped down from the battlements onto the walkway. For a few seconds, the defenders had deserted their posts, blinded by the smoke. It was a fatal mistake. Behind Ludolf came a stream of knights.

Like ink slowly filling a phial, a mass of crusader shields, adorned with blood-red crosses, spread along the ramparts. They raised a banner on top of the wall and advanced in both directions, swords and spears bristling. Within hours, the city had fallen. Soon, headless corpses lay strewn across the streets and in the doorways of houses. Severed heads, hands and arms littered the ground. The crusaders staggered over the multitude of bodies. Some of the foot soldiers and squires set to work slitting open the stomachs of the dead. Plunging their hands into the still warm entrails, they searched for jewels and coins their victims might have swallowed.

Meanwhile, the leaders of the crusade gathered in the Church of the Holy Sepulchre, reputed to be the very site of Christ's crucifixion and the tomb from which he was resurrected. And there, dripping in blood and gore, they prayed to God and gave thanks for their miraculous triumph. The date was 15 July 1099. A day that changed the course of history.

The scale of the First Crusade was unprecedented. Crusader armies from across Europe faced Muslim armies drawn from the Middle East, the Asian Steppe lands and North Africa. Its brutality was also unprecedented, and shocking even by medieval standards. As such, it has been condemned by countless observers, including the modern papacy. Yet it reshaped the Middle Ages and served as the crucible for the modern world.

But why did it happen? The answer is that it began as a mission to rescue an ancient empire. That empire was Byzantium. For many people the word is vague, perhaps conjuring up images of a semi-oriental state with convoluted bureaucracies and politics. Yet this does it little justice. It was, in fact, the Eastern Roman Empire that survived through the Dark Ages and into the early medieval period. The term 'Byzantine' is deeply misleading since it was only coined in the sixteenth century and has served to obscure the fact that the Roman state survived for so long. Although the Byzantines spoke Greek rather than Latin, they inherited and maintained Roman culture and institutions – from the existence of a Senate to chariot racing. The Byzantine army was also the direct descendant of the Roman legions and preserved the traditions of a professional army.

At the heart of Byzantium was its capital, Constantinople, now modern Istanbul. Today it may look like a Turkish city but it contains an old city that was once a huge Roman metropolis and the largest city in Europe for nearly 1,000 years. Even today it has the remains of almost as many Roman buildings as Rome itself – towering walls and aqueducts, huge pillared underground cisterns, and churches that still dominate the modern skyline.

For centuries, Byzantium played a critically important part in European history, preserving the Greco-Roman civilisation that was destroyed in the West, and, just as Athens and Sparta had done in their day, protecting Europe against the onslaught of oriental empires, from the Persians to the Arabs. Yet in the eleventh century, this changed. Byzantium was challenged by the rise of a new superpower – the Seljuk Turks – whose empire stretched from India to the Mediterranean. A major war, between the Byzantines and the Turks was fought between 1068 and 1071, which acted as the precursor and cause of the First Crusade.[1] Both events were together, in effect, a world war. This book tells that story.

---

1    This war has been strangely neglected by historians with relatively little written about it.

# PART I

# The Forgotten Empire

*Eleventh-century Byzantine shield*

# 1

# A NEW HERO

In the autumn of 1067, a young Byzantine general stood on trial before the Senate in Constantinople. The charge was treason. If convicted, the penalty would be death. Most people in his place would have been shivering with fear. But not him. A senator recalled that: *"He was tall and his broad chest gave him a fine appearance, and he seemed to breathe nobility."*[1] His name was Romanus Diogenes.

The Senate house was a large and ancient Roman basilica at the eastern end of the city. Within its echoing chambers, Romanus faced the assembled rows of senators. They regarded him thoughtfully, knowing that he had an enviable reputation. He was said to be the best general in the army. The soldiers loved him. His enemies feared him.

They asked him whether it was true that he had planned a rebellion. He said it was – he had planned a rebellion of the western army against the Emperor. Asked why, he replied simply that the empire was on the brink of disaster. Something had to be done. The Emperor and his government had done nothing to stop the barbarians from burning Byzantine cities in the east. Time was running out. He didn't plead for their forgiveness. The senators were silent. They knew that he spoke the truth.

## The World of Romanus Diogenes

Romanus was an aristocrat from a family with huge estates in Cappadocia – the heartland of the Byzantine Empire at this time. His father had been a senior general in the army, although thirty years earlier, disliking the vain and incompetent rule of the then Emperor, he had been implicated in a conspiracy against him and committed suicide rather than face torture.

Surprisingly, this disgrace didn't stop his son from pursuing a successful career in the army, attaining the rank of Vestarch by his thirties, equivalent to a senior general. In Constantine X's reign, Romanus was stationed in the west at Serdica[2] and had fought successfully against Byzantium's enemies along the Danube. He became a hero of the western army and was held in high regard by his enemies because of his military abilities, so much so that the Hungarians were keen to join his rebellion.

The senators were surprised and impressed by the honesty of this young general. But before we learn their verdict, why had Romanus chosen to risk his life in a rebellion? The answer lies far away in the east, in Cappadocia, where his family had lived for centuries.

Several months before his rebellion, Caesarea, a city close to Romanus' own estates in Cappadocia, had been sacked by marauding Turks. It was a prosperous Byzantine city in what is now modern-day Turkey. A thousand years ago it would have been Greek speaking and its central square would have been a bustling marketplace full of agricultural produce and livestock from the surrounding countryside. It was famous for its textile industry as well as weapon production. In the eleventh century, the city was used to a peaceful existence. It

---

2    Modern Sofia, the capital of Bulgaria.

had last been attacked by the Arabs in AD 726, and since then its walls had fallen into disrepair, so that it fell without much resistance to a force of several thousand Turkish horsemen.

The sack of the city would have been a truly horrific sight. The Turks were not regular soldiers but nomadic tribesmen from the Asian Steppe lands, only recently converted to Islam and a primitive people unused to seeing cities like Caesarea. We can imagine that they took delight in an orgy of killing, raping and enslaving its citizens who must have been easy victims. A senator described the pillage of the city's main church: *"The barbarians… broke into the shrine of the illustrious hierarch, Saint Basil, and tore it apart, looting all the sacred furnishings. They even broke open the saint's tomb."*[xii] A great Byzantine city was virtually obliterated.

Caesarea wasn't the first Byzantine city to be sacked by the Seljuks. They had sacked others further to the east, in Armenia and eastern Anatolia. But Caesarea was different. It was in the heartland of the empire and its destruction signalled that events were spiralling out of hand. Something needed to be done.

But the imperial government wasn't doing anything. The old Emperor Constantine X Doukas had died six months earlier, leaving government in the hands of his widow, the Empress Eudocia, still in her thirties. Her husband had made her vow, before the Patriarch of Constantinople himself, never to remarry. The heir to the throne was her eldest son, Michael, a bookish and unworldly teenager who no one considered either old enough or suitable to be Emperor. The senators and the people of Constantinople were increasingly talking of the need to find a soldier to confront the Turks. But who should that be?

Let us return to Romanus' trial. The senators were impressed by his honesty when he admitted his guilt. They decided to excuse him from execution and to exile him to an island. However, this lucky escape was just the beginning. His unexpected pardon catapulted him into the limelight and he rapidly became a celebrity in the capital. His *'youthful spirit and nobility'*[iii] became the talk of the town. Wasn't a general as selfless and brave as him just what the empire needed? A senator recorded: *"Others who had no direct knowledge of him came to know him from those who did, and what they heard made them love him."*[iv]

And it wasn't just the senators and the people of Constantinople who were impressed. The Empress asked to see him. Romanus was taken to the Great Palace, a fabled myriad of beautifully decorated buildings spread over many acres, now almost completely submerged beneath modern Istanbul.

He was brought to the throne room where the Empress sat waiting for him. He stood before her. It seems to have been love at first sight. Apparently moved to tears, she immediately pardoned him of all his crimes and released him without punishment. But it soon became apparent that she had other plans for him. No sooner had he returned to his native Cappadocia than he received a message from her. She recalled him to the capital and asked him to become commander-in-chief of the army. From facing execution to this was no small feat. But it was to be followed by something even more spectacular.

While Caesarea was a smoking ruin, and Turkish tribesmen were closing in on Byzantium's walled cities of Edessa and Antioch in northern Syria, the Empress and the Senate in Constantinople had heard of something even more worrying. There was news that the Seljuk Turkish Sultan, Alp Arslan, was marching with an army into Armenia, which he had seized from Byzantine control a few years before, and he was now planning a full-scale invasion of the empire.

There was panic in the capital. The people were clamouring for the Empress to appoint a general capable of leading the army against the Turks. She called her high council to deliberate what to do. Although she had sworn a vow before the Patriarch never to remarry, she proposed that in this dire state of emergency an Emperor must be appointed. Suitable candidates were discussed. These included Nicephorus Botaneiates, a highly regarded general and the governor of Antioch in the east, who was already engaged in a successful defence of the city against the Turks. But it soon became clear that Eudocia had Romanus in mind, and given his recent rise to popularity, the decision was not difficult. There was no resistance in the Senate to his being made Emperor, not even from the Empress's own relations, the powerful Doukas family and the rightful heirs to the throne (Eudocia's own young son, Michael, was next in line to be Emperor). She called Romanus to the Great Palace to tell him the news.

We will never know the true story of the relations between Romanus and Eudocia. Were they already having an affair before she made him Emperor? Certainly, it was extremely convenient that Romanus was not married at the time. Previously, he had been married to the daughter of a Bulgarian noble who died of an unrecorded cause in the 1060s, perhaps dying in childbirth since they had only one son, Constantine.

Contemporary sources hint that Eudocia was physically attracted to Romanus, and their marriage seems to have been a happy one with two children born in rapid succession. But it shouldn't be forgotten that Eudocia was also a tough politician herself, and by marrying Romanus she secured her own political independence, providing of course she could control her new husband.

## THE CORONATION OF ROMANUS DIOGENES

On 1 January 1068, Romanus was anointed Emperor in the great cathedral of Constantinople, Hagia Sophia, which still dominates the skyline of modern Istanbul. As he stood on the purple stone reserved for imperial coronations,[3] the Empress would have been at his side. They must have been a handsome couple. Eudocia was a determined woman in the prime of her life. Beside her, Romanus would have looked every inch the tall, strong soldier. Around them, the great and the good of Byzantium looked on, smiling and elated that now, at long last, a soldier was on the throne.

But there were some who weren't smiling. These were the Doukai (Doukas in the singular), the wealthiest and most powerful family in the empire. The last Emperor had been a Doukas (Constantine X) and, not surprisingly, the Doukai saw Romanus' promotion to Emperor as a threat to their future. The Doukai were led by John Doukas, the last Emperor's brother. His title was Caesar, a 'grace and favour' rank conferred by the Byzantines on people considered second only to the Emperor (we shall refer to him as Caesar John, as contemporaries did). When his brother died in 1067, he had acted as regent for Constantine X's teenage son and heir to the throne, Michael. Romanus' astonishing promotion was particularly galling because it had been done without his prior consultation.

As Romanus was to learn, Caesar John was the worst enemy anyone could have. Well versed in the politics of the court, he was adept at every political stratagem. He was also utterly ruthless, focused only on the preservation of power for

---

3    Visitors to Hagia Sophia today can still see the purple marble embedded in the floor.

the Doukai. Like his brother, the former Constantine X, he didn't care about the fate of the eastern provinces so long as the Doukai maintained their hold on government. Famously bad-tempered and vindictive, it would be no exaggeration to say that Caesar John hated Romanus and felt bitterly betrayed by the Empress.

With enemies both internally and externally, the task facing Romanus must have seemed daunting indeed. But no one was more eager to confront the crisis that faced Byzantium. This had been developing for decades and it is to this subject that we must now turn.

# 2

# THE CRISIS OF BYZANTIUM

The term 'Byzantine'[4] is misleading. The Byzantines called themselves Romans and their empire was the eastern half of the Roman Empire that survived the fall of Rome. As Roman civilisation in Western Europe was trampled underfoot by Germanic tribes in a period known as the Dark Ages, the Eastern Mediterranean continued to prosper. Great ancient cities like Constantinople, Antioch and Alexandria thrived with hundreds of thousands of inhabitants. The Roman army survived in the East as a professional military organisation, unique in the world outside China. In the sixth century, there was even a counter-attack to recover the West. The Emperor Justinian reconquered Italy, and Rome itself, from the Goths.

However, Byzantium was nearly destroyed by the birth of Islam and the huge Arab conquests in the seventh century.[5] Just managing to survive this onslaught, its ethnicity changed from being a heterogeneous empire with Egyptians, Syrians and Africans among its citizens to becoming predominantly

---

4   The term Byzantine was first coined in the sixteenth century by a German historian, Hieronymus Wolf.
5   The Arab Umayyad dynasty ruled an empire stretching from India to Spain.

Greek. In the tenth century, it underwent a renaissance, led by a new military aristocracy. Soldier-Emperors regained the military initiative from the Arabs, pushing them out of Cilicia and recovering the great city of Antioch on the Syrian frontier. It entered its most fascinating phase: a survivor from the ancient world that had reinvented itself as a medieval superpower.

At the heart of Byzantium was the fabled city of Constantinople. The dream of every Viking warrior was to see this city, or Miklagard, as they called it. It was just as awe-inspiring as ancient Rome. Its land walls were the most impressive feat of defensive construction in both the ancient and medieval worlds. Twelve metres high, with ninety-six towers and nine gateways, they formed a double set of walls standing behind a wide moat. Within the city stood the towering church of Hagia Sophia, built by the Emperor Justinian in the sixth century, and the largest building in Europe for nearly a thousand years. With a dome measuring over one hundred feet wide, it was a triumph of engineering. There were dozens of other great stone churches, huge aqueducts, a vast hippodrome, a sprawling imperial palace and hundreds of statues from antiquity adorning the forums and streets of the city. Its population in the eleventh century numbered over a quarter of a million, ten times larger than that of any other city in Europe. As one crusader recounted: *Oh what a noble and beautiful city is Constantinople! How many monasteries and palaces it contains, constructed with wonderful skill!*[v]

Byzantium's revival in the tenth century was based on a combination of economic and military success. The Byzantine economy was considerably more sophisticated and developed than that in the West. This is hardly surprising considering its economic legacy from the ancient world. For example, the

Byzantine gold coin, the *nomisma*, was the 'dollar of the Middle Ages', and had no equivalent in Western Europe. Byzantine coinage made trade easier, both within and outside the Byzantine Empire, than in the more primitive Frankish, German and English economies. In addition, levels of literacy were far higher in Byzantium than in the West, helping to promote trade and manufacturing. Archaeological evidence[vi] uncovered over the last forty years has shown that the number and size of Byzantine towns was growing fast in the tenth and eleventh centuries with rapidly increasing production of glass, pottery and textiles.

## THE MEDIEVAL BYZANTINE ARMY

But the most striking aspect of Byzantium's revival lay with its army. In the tenth century, this was probably the largest and best in the world outside China. The direct descendant of the Roman legions, the secret of its success lay with the fusion of provincial levies and centralised professional soldiers. The provincial armies mirrored the empire's division into provinces called 'themes'[6] each with its own army under a local commander (strategus or dux). The centralised professional troops were elite regiments, collectively referred to as the *'tagmata'* (meaning regiment in Greek).

The most prominent of the *tagmata* were the cavalry regiments called the Scholae and the Excubitors, which became the shock troops of the Byzantine army, including the famous *cataphracts*.[7] We have an extensive description of them in a military treatise written by the tenth-century Byzantine soldier-

---

6   The etymology of the Greek word 'thema' is unclear but it possibly referred to a 'list' of soldiers.
7   From the Greek 'Kataphractoi' meaning completely enclosed.

Emperor, Nikephorus Phokas.[vii] They were exceptionally heavily armoured cavalry, wearing chain mail or lamellar armour from head to foot, including a chain-mail face guard, with slits for the eyes, which gave them a particularly intimidating appearance. Wedge-shaped formations of 500 cavalry were used to charge and break the enemy at strategic points. These soldiers were game changers in the tenth century, enabling the Byzantines to defeat Vikings coming from the north and the Arabs in the south. The Arabs were particularly intimidated by the cataphracts *"who advanced on horses which seemed to have no legs"* owing to the horses' armoured coats, and their riders *"whose helmets and garments were of iron like their swords"*.[viii]

Most important of all was a strong military culture deeply embedded in Byzantine society, especially in Anatolia, which had been an area of intense fighting with the Arabs since the seventh century. While the army was divided into two forces – one in the west and one in the east, each with its own commander[8] – it was the much larger and battle-hardened eastern army that dominated Byzantine politics. It had a military aristocracy, concentrated in Cappadocia, that was somewhat similar to the Prussian Junker class that effectively controlled the German army in the years leading to the First World War. In the tenth century, this aristocracy reached the peak of its power when two generals from the eastern army were made Emperors – Nicephorus Phocas (963–69)[9] and John Tzimiskes (969–76).

The results on the battlefield were spectacular in this period. The Arabs were pushed back into Syria. The empire was expanded in aggressive offensives, with the re-conquest

---

8    The commanders of the eastern and western armies were called Domestikos or Domestics.

9    Known as 'The White Death of the Saracens' on account of his many victories over the Arabs.

of Crete, Cyprus, Tarsus and Antioch. This Cappadocian aristocracy devoted themselves completely to the art of war. Pride in martial pursuits dominated Byzantine society just as it did any militaristic society. Contemporary sources record that whenever Nicephorus Phocas was not campaigning, he used his spare time to drill his troops – *"…he* [the Emperor Nicephorus Phocas] *trained* [his troops] *in daily exercises as thoroughly as possible in the arts of war…"*[ix]

## The Reign of Basil II and the Decline of the Byzantine Army

But by the 1060s, the Byzantine army had shrunk to a fraction of what it had been in the tenth century, and the military aristocracy that had made it into the best fighting machine in Europe had been humbled. The causes of this can be traced to the actions of one man: the Emperor Basil II (976–1025).

Menacingly known as the 'Bulgar-slayer',[10] when he acceded to the throne at the tender age of eighteen, Basil II was immediately confronted by major rebellions led by jealous generals in the eastern army, who regarded him as a weak and callow youth. This view was quickly disproved. Basil defeated the rebels using the western army, which remained loyal to him, as well as mercenaries, in particular the newly created Varangian Guard, consisting of Rus Vikings from the Viking-controlled principality of Kiev.

But Basil's next step was to prove disastrous for Byzantium. Not surprisingly, having only just survived the rebellions of the eastern army, he wanted to reduce its power. Although he

---

10 His reputation for brutality was based on his allegedly blinding 14,000 Bulgarian prisoners of war.

didn't disband it completely, he imprisoned its Cappadocian leaders and cut back its numbers by commuting military service in return for tax payments. This proved popular with the local populations who were enjoying a period of unparalleled economic prosperity after the defeat of the Arabs. But the result for the army was that it became smaller and smaller.

He also worked to undermine the power and wealth of the Cappadocian aristocracy by curbing its ability to take over peasants' land. There had been a growing feudalisation of Anatolian society in the tenth century which had greatly strengthened the military resources of the Cappadocian magnates. Basil put this into reverse by passing a law in 996, restricting them from acquiring peasants' land. He followed this up with another law, called the *Allelengyon,* stipulating that they would have to make up the shortfalls in tax on the part of peasants unable to pay. This stopped the poorer peasants coming under their sway. The Cappadocian aristocracy never threatened Basil again.

Basil's next step was to make up for the shrinking eastern army with mercenaries. The Varangians became widely used as the army's main shock troops.[11] This meant that the native Byzantine army started to lose its cutting edge in equipment and tactics. Particularly damaging was the demise of the Byzantine cavalry. In Nicephorus Phocas' army, the famous cataphracts had been the elite troops. But by the end of Basil II's reign there is no record that they existed any more.

---

11   Whose roll call included Vikings such as Harald Hardrada, the future King of Norway, killed in 1066 at the Battle of Stamford Bridge.

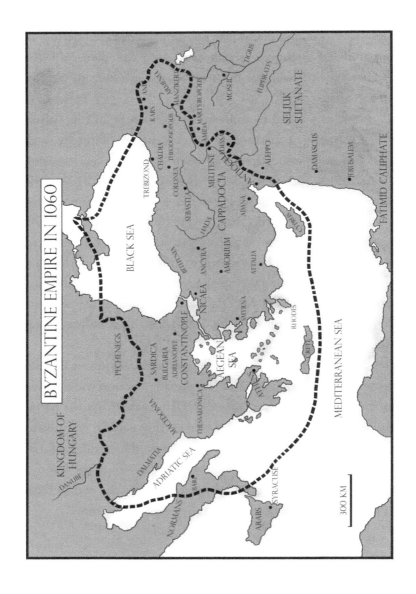

BYZANTINE EMPIRE IN 1060

## BASIL II'S SUCCESSORS

Paradoxically, when Basil II died in 1025, the empire had never seemed so powerful. But this was an illusion created by the absence of dangerous new enemies. Basil had been lucky enough not to face any serious external military threats. His only challenge was a revived Bulgar state, which he crushed relatively easily. His successors were not so lucky. After his death, new enemies appeared from the Asian Steppes – the Pechenegs from the north and the Turks in the east. Now, an effective army was needed. But Basil's successors were still more afraid of military rebellions than external enemies, and continued his policy of preferring mercenaries over native troops.

As the eleventh century rolled on, mercenaries came to dominate the army. In addition to the Varangians, Norman cavalry were first employed in the 1030s in the wars in southern Italy against the Arabs. The Byzantines hired young men in search of fortune and adventure from northern Europe. The regular Byzantine army got smaller and smaller as military service was increasingly commuted. A particularly damaging example of this occurred in 1053, when Constantine IX disbanded the provincial armies in Armenia to boost his tax revenues. This proved disastrous as Armenia became the front line facing the Seljuk Turkish advance. By the 1060s, the provincial armies that had formed the backbone of the glorious army of the tenth century had largely ceased to exist. Indeed, the distinction between centralised soldiers (*tagmata*) and provincial soldiers (*themata*) had faded to the point that Byzantine sources in the later eleventh century refer to all native Byzantine soldiers as 'tagmatic', simply meaning regiments.

Basil II's legacy was a poisoned chalice in every way. Not only did he undermine the Byzantine army but he also died childless and seemed not to care about his succession. Almost nothing is known about his personal life and it remains a mystery why he never married. The result was decades of incompetent rule by a string of successors whose only claim to power was to be related to him. Basil II belonged to a ruling dynasty founded in the ninth century by Basil I.[12] Consequently, on Basil II's death, the imperial crown passed first to his elderly brother, Constantine, who lived for only three years, and then to Constantine's eldest daughter, Zoe, who ruled until 1055 with three successive husbands as Emperor – all three hopelessly ineffective and none of them soldiers. In 1034, the emir of Aleppo defeated the hitherto invincible Byzantine army for the first time in living memory. Incensed by this humiliation, the Anatolian aristocracy considered rebellion. As already mentioned, one of them, Romanus Diogenes' father, was arrested and committed suicide. In the end there was no rebellion and the army continued to waste away.

During the reign of Zoe's last husband, Constantine IX Monomachus (1042–55), it became increasingly clear that the empire didn't have the military muscle to combat its new enemies. Although a Viking Rus attack on Constantinople was trounced by the Byzantine navy in 1043, this was only because of the use of Greek fire,[13] which caught the Vikings unawares and burnt their fleet. Otherwise, the empire's army struggled to contain the increasing attacks of Steppe nomads who hurled themselves at the empire's frontiers along the Danube in the west and in Armenia in the east.

---

12  The House of Macedon had ignominious origins. Basil I was a peasant supposedly from Macedonia, who murdered the reigning Emperor, Michael III, and seduced his wife.

13  A petrol-based incendiary flamethrower device.

The government also started to run out of money. While Basil II had left the state coffers overflowing with gold on his death in 1025, by the middle of the eleventh century, the cost of paying for mercenaries to fight the empire's new enemies was bankrupting the government. Constantine IX took the easy way out and resorted to devaluation of the currency. He devalued the *nomisma*, reducing its gold content to 81%. He also minted a lightweight gold coin, the *tetarteron*, which he used to pay the growing number of mercenaries he recruited to fight the Pechenegs and Seljuks, devaluing it to 73% of its original gold content.

Finally, in 1056, a potential turning point was reached when the House of Macedon was finally extinguished with the death of the last of Basil's heirs – Zoe's younger daughter, Theodora (Zoe herself had died in 1055). This created a make or break chance for a new political order. The powerful aristocratic families from Anatolia were quick to respond. The Comnenus, Doukas and Katakolon families joined together and marched on Constantinople where they made one of their own Emperor: Isaac Comnenus.

Isaac was the first Emperor with military experience since Basil II, and, at first, it looked as if a strong military government would be restored. He immediately started to reform the army and fiscal system. But Isaac struggled to keep the different aristocratic families happy. Some started to oppose him. And then his luck turned when this intelligent and well-intentioned Emperor fell gravely ill. Physically weakened, he didn't have the strength to continue to battle both internally and externally. He retired to a monastery, where he died soon after, and handed power in 1059 to Constantine X Doukas.

Constantine X's reign (1059–67) accelerated Byzantium's decline. Too concerned about securing the support of the other aristocratic families to care about the empire's plight, he spent his days enjoying the luxuries of Constantinople and playing court politics. Perhaps surprisingly, the Anatolian aristocracy, underestimating the Seljuk threat, joined him. They abandoned the defence of the eastern provinces to parade in the streets of Constantinople, jostling for pre-eminence in a bloated imperial court and bureaucracy.

Basil II's legacy had proved to be far worse than he could possibly have imagined. It might not have been as bad had Byzantium's neighbours been as weak as they were during his reign. But the Emperors of the eleventh century were not so lucky. For right on their doorstep had suddenly appeared a new superpower – the empire of the Seljuk Turks.

# 3

# BARBARIANS
# AT THE GATES

J ust as the Western Roman Empire had crumbled 600 years
earlier beneath wave after wave of barbarian invaders, so
Byzantium in the eleventh century faced a seemingly endless
onslaught of barbarians battering at its gates. Indeed, so many
new enemies appeared out of nowhere in the 1040s–60s, that
many pious Byzantines were convinced God was punishing
them. Portents of doom were superstitiously seen everywhere,
from a major earthquake in 1063, which damaged the
Byzantine cities of Antioch and Nicaea, to the appearance of
Halley's Comet in 1066.

What was really happening was that the empire was being
buffeted by the migrations of several nomadic tribes from the
central Asian Steppe lands. They were all of Turkish descent and
all of them ultimately came from the East. The first onslaught
struck at Byzantium's north-western frontier. In the winter of
1046–47, the Pechenegs, one of several Turkish tribes, poured
across the frozen Danube in their thousands, and during the
years up to 1053 they fought a fierce and costly war with the
Byzantines, eventually ending in a peace treaty that allowed
them to settle in Byzantine territory in modern-day Bulgaria.

In 1065, a powerful force of Oghuz Turks, similar to their Seljuk cousins and more formidable warriors than the Pechenegs, also crossed the Danube. They were resisted by both Byzantine and Pecheneg forces, but nevertheless succeeded in ravaging most of the Balkans up to the great Byzantine walled city of Thessalonica in northern Greece. Fortunately for the Byzantines, the Oghuz Turks fell prey to a devastating plague and fled back north across the Danube.

In Italy, things also went from bad to worse. In the 1040s, the Normans had started to wrest control of southern Italy from the Byzantines. The Normans are usually associated with northern Europe – in particular their conquest of Saxon England in 1066 – but a group of Norman adventurers had joined the Byzantine army in the 1030s to fight against the Arabs, only to revolt against their paymasters and set up their own principality in Apulia. The Normans had a particularly effective cavalry charge. Frequently described by Byzantine sources, this was used to devastating effect on all of their opponents. Indeed, it would be no exaggeration to say that it was the medieval equivalent of the German Blitzkrieg in the Second World War and would later be a major contributor to the success of the First Crusade. By 1067, when Romanus stood trial, the Normans had reduced Byzantine territory in Italy to its last stronghold at Bari.

But the greatest threat came from the east – and it was from an enemy that had developed one of the most paradoxical empires in history – the empire of the Seljuk Turks.

## The Rise of the Seljuks

The origins of Seljuk power lie with the charismatic ability of a man called Seljuk, who rose to prominence in the late

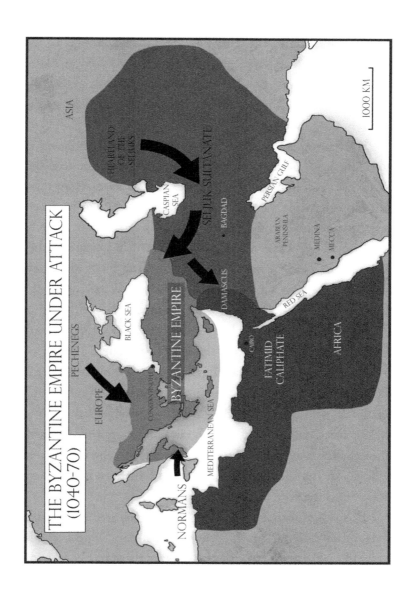

THE BYZANTINE EMPIRE UNDER ATTACK (1040-70)

1000 KM

ASIA

HEARTLAND OF THE SELJUKS

SELJUK SULTANATE

CASPIAN SEA

BAGDAD

PERSIAN GULF

ARABIAN PENINSULA

MEDINA

MECCA

PECHENEGS

BLACK SEA

BYZANTINE EMPIRE

DAMASCUS

RED SEA

EUROPE

CONSTANTINOPLE

CAIRO

FATIMID CALIPHATE

AFRICA

MEDITERRANEAN SEA

NORMANS

tenth century. He was an Oghuz Turk, and at that time the Oghuz Turks were a group of nomads living around the Volga River. Originally coming from Mongolia, the homeland of all the Steppe nomads, the Turks were ethnically similar to the Huns of the late Roman period and the future Mongols of the thirteenth century. All of these Steppe nomads essentially shared a similar ethnicity and culture, separated only by the different ages they lived in.

The first mention of Seljuk comes in the late tenth century when he led a group of Oghuz Turks east into modern-day Kazakhstan, fleeing from his masters, the Khazars. Entering a Muslim-ruled area, he converted to Islam. Although we know very little about him, he must have had a charismatic style of leadership for he was conspicuously successful in attracting other Oghuz Turks to join his clan and persuading them to convert to Islam, so much so that contemporaries started to call the growing number of Oghuz Turkish nomads who converted to Islam 'Turkmen' (the term historians also use to refer to them). This distinguished them from the rest of the Oghuz Turks.

Ironically, it was defeat that first put the Seljuks on the path to victory. In 1034, Seljuk's grandsons, Tughril and Chaghri, who ruled jointly (Seljuk himself died around 1009), were defeated by the Qarakhanids, another Turkish nomadic dynasty. The Seljuks fled south into the Ghaznavid Empire, an Islamic Persian state in modern Iran. It was there they found the secret of their success.

This was to rule by means of what amounted to a mafia-style protection racket. In other words, the Seljuks would normally take control of cities by making them pay protection money rather than installing their own government and rulers. They could do this because of their extreme mobility. Seljuk warriors could appear out of nowhere, having travelled hundreds of miles in a matter of days on their tireless ponies. For the Seljuks were the masters of light cavalry warfare. Wearing little body armour and carrying a short, normally slightly curved sabre and sometimes a javelin, the Turkmen warriors relied on their powerful bows. The Turkish bow was beautifully built, recurved in shape and constructed in three parts: a thin central stave of wood laminated with sinew on the back and horn on the underside. This composite construction was designed for power and speed, with the warrior able to use the recurved shape for a powerful draw, repeatedly quickly, and aimed in any direction. According to a Byzantine source,[x] when a Seljuk warrior shot his arrow: *"...the arrow in its course strikes either rider or horse, fired with such a tremendous force that it passes clean through the body."*

Equestrian skills were paramount. The Seljuks rode with a short stirrup which allowed them to put the rider's weight over the horse's shoulder instead of squarely on its back. This gave them better control for archery and facilitated their style of hit-and-run fighting. Seljuk warriors hovered within bowshot of their enemy, peppering them with arrows, and when charged they would take flight, firing arrows backwards in the style called the 'Parthian shot' by the Romans.[14] They would continue these tactics until their enemy was so worn down that they could charge home with their sabres. If no such opportunity presented itself, they would continue to harass their enemy for days without offering battle, waiting for a suitable ambush or making surprise attacks on the enemy's camp or outposts.

In contrast, the Ghaznavid army used heavily armoured troops, even including elephants, a strategy copied from their Indian neighbours. This type of army proved far too slow to

---

14   In reference to the Parthian Empire, the Iranian successor state to the Achaemenid Persians.

pursue and confront the Seljuk war bands. The Ghaznavids had little experience of Steppe nomad warfare and exhausted Ghaznavid armies criss-crossed Khurasan, vainly trying to pin down the Seljuks to a pitched battle.

Yet, in order to win battles, the Turkmen had to fight at close quarters at some point. Finally, in 1040, this happened at the Battle of Dandanqan. Chaghri, the main Seljuk leader, chose the timing of his attack with typical Seljuk cunning, waiting until the Ghaznavid army was actually locked in a quarrel between its own soldiers over access to a water well, in order to ambush and completely rout them. The Ghaznavid Sultan, Mas'ud, was killed as he fled and the Seljuks took over complete control of the Ghaznavid Empire.

Next was western Iran. While the Seljuks at this time had two leaders, Tughril and Chaghri, it was Tughril who rose to prominence by conquering western Iran and Iraq, leaving Chaghri in charge of the east. Tughril's invasion of Iran used the same formula that had worked so well against the Ghaznavids. He led his growing hordes of nomadic Turkmen to force cities to pledge allegiance in return for their protection. The Iranian political infrastructure was too fragmented to be able to offer effective resistance, consisting of a multitude of principalities nominally subject to the ethnically Iranian Buyid dynasty but in fact self-governing and often in conflict with each other. The Seljuk method of government suited them reasonably well, since once these local Iranian and Kurdish princes had sworn their allegiance to the Seljuks, they were left alone. In this way, the Seljuks allowed the underlying political infrastructures in Iran and Iraq to remain largely intact.

But the interaction between the primitive Turkmen and the sophisticated Muslim populations living in Iran and Iraq was still tense and difficult. The latter normally ended up paying taxes or tribute in order to continue their lives undisturbed, and while the Turks brought large numbers of livestock with them to boost the local economies by providing milk, meat and wool,[15] there is little doubt that the local populations regarded them with fear and trepidation.

Tughril knew he couldn't allow this style of rule in Iraq, the heartland of Islam, without provoking a more formidable resistance. So, he tried to ensure that the Turkmen behaved with respect for the local population by giving them what they wanted – grazing land for their flocks, and the protection money he extorted from local populations. This worked well, and soon Tughril arrived with his hordes of Turkmen before the gates of Baghdad itself, the great holy city and seat of the Sunni Abbasid Caliph. There the fragmented political situation in Iraq continued to favour him. The long-standing Sunni Abbasid Caliph, al-Qa'im (1031–67), disliked the weak rule of the Shi'ite Buyids. Tughril took full advantage of these internal divisions when he threatened to take Baghdad by force, and the Caliph persuaded the Buyid forces to flee the city. He entered it peacefully in 1055 and was proclaimed Sultan by the Caliph. The Seljuks had come of age. But they had a new enemy to face.

This was the powerful Fatimid caliphate based in Egypt. The Fatimids were Arabs originally from Algeria, who had extended their dominion eastwards, conquering Tunisia, Libya, Egypt and the Levant in the tenth century. Not only were they the only other major Muslim power opposed to the Seljuks, but they were also Shia, so doctrinally opposed to the

---

15   On a more positive note, it has been suggested that the Seljuk flocks boosted the GDP of Iran. For example, a single Turkmen family may have had around 50 sheep, meaning that a 5,000-strong war band could have been accompanied by around 100,000 sheep! – assuming two to three warriors in each family.

Sunni Seljuks.[16] The Fatimids took Baghdad from the Seljuks in 1058, although the city was quickly recovered by the Seljuks the next year. Thereafter, the Seljuks' main objective was to rid Syria and the Levant of the Fatimids.

## THE PARADOX OF THE SELJUK EMPIRE

The Seljuk Empire was balanced precariously on a paradox: its military strength depended on the Turkmen tribesmen and yet these nomads had no interest in empire-building. They disliked Tughril's 'gentrification' when he renounced the nomadic way of life in favour of the sophisticated and literate court in Baghdad. They disliked it even more when poets praised him in an Arabic language which neither they nor he could understand. But most of all, the Turkmen hated the arid Iraqi countryside which was unsuitable for their flocks.

Tughril knew that to survive he had to manage the conflicting needs of the Turkmen and the Caliph in Baghdad. His power depended on the military might of the Turkmen but their raiding and pillaging would not be tolerated by the Caliph. Indeed, the Caliph regularly protested about their unruly behaviour in the Iraqi countryside outside Baghdad. To retain the Caliph's support, Tughril had to withdraw his forces from Baghdad in 1057. He needed grazing lands suitable for the millions of Turkmen sheep and he needed cities that could be pillaged and burnt. Where could he take them?

The answer was Byzantine Armenia.

---

16   The original cause of division between Shia and Sunni Muslims was over the choice of a successor to the Prophet Muhammad in AD 632, and whether such was chosen by God or by his followers.

# 4

# THE FIRST SELJUK ATTACKS ON BYZANTIUM

In 1048, the Seljuk Turks made their first significant attack on Byzantine Armenia. A large force of Turkmen led by one of Tughril's emirs, Asan, appeared in Vaspuracan (Eastern Armenia). The attack could not have happened at a worse time for the Byzantines since the Emperor Constantine IX Monomachus, pursuing a policy of fiscal austerity, had disbanded the regular army in the Iberian theme (Western Armenia).

For the Byzantines, Armenia should have made a good buffer state with the Seljuks. Its mountainous countryside was difficult terrain for invading armies and it had several strongly fortified cities in the form of Ani, Kars and Manzikert. Its population also had a robust military tradition and provided particularly good foot soldiers for the Byzantine armies. But the Byzantines failed to take advantage of these opportunities. The main reason was mutual antipathy. Armenia had a long history of independence, having only fallen under Byzantine control at the beginning of the eleventh century in Basil II's reign, and its nobility were lukewarm at best in accepting Byzantine authority. There were also serious religious tensions.

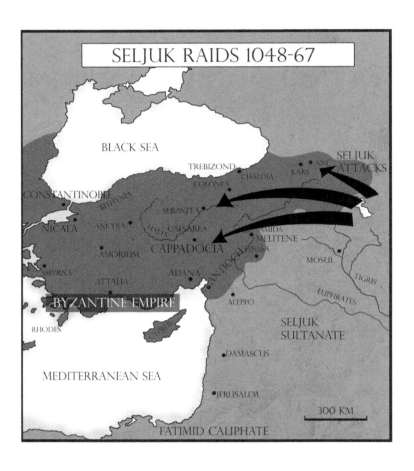

## SELJUK RAIDS 1048-67

BLACK SEA

SELJUK ATTACKS

TREBIZOND

CHALDIA

KARS ANI

COLONEA

CONSTANTINOPLE

BITHYNIA

SEBASTEA

NICAEA

ANCYRA

HALYS

CAESAREA

AMORIUM

CAPPADOCIA

AMIDA

MELITENE

EDESSA

SMYRNA

ADANA

ANTIOCH

MOSUL

ATTALIA

TIGRIS

BYZANTINE EMPIRE

EUPHRATES

RHODES

CYPRUS

ALEPPO

SELJUK SULTANATE

DAMASCUS

MEDITERRANEAN SEA

JERUSALEM

300 KM

FATIMID CALIPHATE

Although Christian, the Armenian Church had never recognised Constantinople's authority, and many Byzantines regarded them as heretics.

In spite of all of this, initially at least, the Byzantines put up a remarkably effective resistance against the Seljuks. This was essentially due to the efforts of one man: Katakolon Kekaumenos. A highly experienced soldier in the regular army, who had fought against the Arabs in Sicily and the Rus along the Danube, he was given the governorship of Ani in the 1040s. In 1048, hearing of the Seljuk advance, he hastily put together a scratch force of Varangian and Frankish mercenaries together with what Byzantine troops he could find. This small force defeated the invading Seljuk army by tricking the Turks into thinking the Byzantine camp had been left unguarded. As they plundered it, he attacked them and sent them fleeing in panic.

But the next year, in 1049, the Turks attacked again with a larger war band, led by a Seljuk prince, Ibrahim Inal. This time, things didn't go quite as well. Katakolon couldn't prevent them from sacking the important Armenian city of Artze. However, he managed to ambush them as they retreated, and although the battle was indecisive, the Turks withdrew from Armenia in the knowledge that although the Byzantine army was quite weak, Katakolon was a soldier to be reckoned with.

This robust Byzantine defence continued when Tughril himself led an army into Armenia to besiege Manzikert in 1054. The city held out under the leadership of another good Byzantine commander, an Armenian called Basileus Apokapes. Byzantine morale was surprisingly high, with the record of a daring SAS-style raid by a Frankish mercenary on the largest of the Turkish catapults that was causing damage to the city walls: *"The Frank galloped out of the city gates straight* towards the catapult and threw a pot of Greek fire onto the fabrics that protected the wooden machine from Byzantine archers. The siege machine was engulfed in flame."*xi*

The Frank escaped unharmed back into the city. In the face of such determined resistance, Tughril had to concede defeat. Byzantine-Seljuk relations improved when Tughril took Baghdad and became preoccupied with the Fatimid opposition he faced in Syria. In 1055, Tughril made a formal peace treaty with the Byzantine Emperor, Constantine IX, who recognised him as Sultan instead of the Fatimid Sultan, with prayers commemorating him at the mosque in Constantinople.

## THE SELJUK ATTACKS ESCALATE

So far, things seemed to be going better for the Byzantines in the east than in the west where the Pechenegs had occupied most of Bulgaria. But in the late 1050s, the situation became radically worse for the Byzantines. The reason was that, in 1057, Tughril led the bulk of his Turkmen followers north to Armenia and Georgia to divert them from causing trouble in Iraq. Because of this, more and more Turkmen started to mass on the Byzantine borders. Turkish raids into Byzantine Armenia intensified from 1057 onwards in spite of the official Byzantine-Seljuk peace treaty, as Tughril cast a blind eye on the Turkmen depredations.

Unfortunately for the Byzantines, this happened at just the same time as a short civil war in 1057 when Isaac Comnenus was proclaimed Emperor. The problem was that the Anatolian nobles stripped the east of troops in order to advance on Constantinople. In particular, the able general

Katakolon Kekaumenos was a central figure in the uprising and took away his troops who had been successfully defending Armenia.

The result was disastrous. Turkish war bands poured through the open countryside. And this time their attacks took on a new dimension. They bypassed the Armenian strongholds of Ani and Manzikert and invaded the eastern rim of Byzantine Anatolia. For the first time, Greek-speaking Byzantine cities were sacked. In 1057, Coloneia was laid waste. In 1058, Melitene, one of the largest Byzantine cities in Eastern Anatolia, was devastated. In 1059, it was the turn of Sebasteia, a particularly wealthy city and religiously significant since it was the location of a famous shrine of the Forty Martyrs. The Seljuk emir, Samuh, acting independently of Tughril and probably against his wishes, arrived to find that the city was not protected by walls. The Turks hesitated, unable to believe this, and initially mistook the many domes of churches in the city for the tents of a defending army.[xii] When they realised their mistake, they attacked with particular ferocity, massacring its citizens and taking the rest prisoner. They stayed in the area for eight days and reduced the entire city to ashes. The war in the east had entered a new and terrifying phase.

Isaac Comnenus wanted to confront the Turks but he was prevented from sending large-scale reinforcements to the east by the outbreak of war yet again with the Pechenegs in the west. Then his early abdication, due to ill health in 1059, put an end to any hopes for the resolute military action that was needed. In spite of this, Constantine X (the first Doukas Emperor) did send some troops back to the east to stem the Turkmen assaults. Although the surviving records are thin, there is mention that the Byzantines defeated one of the Turkish war bands, killing its leader. By the early 1060s, the Byzantine forces in the east had been strengthened with Frankish and Norman cavalry who at least prevented a complete collapse of the frontier.[17] Nevertheless, it was now clear that the war in the east was starting to pose a serious threat.

## ALP ARSLAN

As the Byzantines dithered under the ineffective leadership of Constantine X, the Seljuk Turks were getting stronger. In 1064, Alp Arslan succeeded Tughril. Previously the Seljuk Empire had been divided into two parts, but now Alp Arslan, already ruler of the eastern half of the Seljuk Empire, united both east and west into a vast single bloc stretching from India to Syria. Like Tughril, Alp Arslan was a formidable leader, respected by the Turkmen and renowned for his archery skills: *"...they say that his arrow never went astray."*[xiii]

Worryingly for the Byzantines, within months of his accession, he led an army of Turkmen north into Byzantine Armenia. But a major war with Byzantium was not his intention. Instead, his concerns were essentially the same as those of Tughril: keeping the Turkmen loyal and driving the Fatimids out of Syria. Byzantine Armenia remained a convenient diversion for the Turkmen.

Indeed, Alp Arslan's advance into Armenia was a show of strength designed to impress the Turkmen, not the Byzantines. However, his actions had unintended consequences that would ignite a full-scale war with Byzantium. At least initially, the blame for this can be attributed to a man called Pangratius,

---

17   One unit of which temporarily joined the Turks showing the unreliability of such mercenaries.

who was the governor of the city of Ani, the capital of Byzantine Armenia. He was little more than a criminal,[xiv] only interested in extorting tax revenues for his own use rather than defending the city. But he had won Constantine X's approval by promising to pay him higher taxes which he did by reducing the city's defences to the bare minimum.

However, Ani was not just a wealthy trading centre but it was also protected by the best fortifications in Armenia and should have been able to hold out against the Turks. Indeed, Alp Arslan didn't even intend to attack it. This only happened because, as he was passing peacefully along the Armenian border, the incompetent and greedy Pangratius ambushed the Seljuk rearguard in the hope of picking up some booty. A large number of Turks were killed which enraged Alp Arslan. He immediately laid siege to the city. Having lost all confidence in Pangratius' ability to resist the Seljuks, a group of its citizens attempted to flee, but when they opened the gates the Turks stormed in. The extent of the slaughter was particularly horrific: "*...they (the Seljuks) took the city by storm, and the slaughter of those inside was beyond telling. For no mercy was shown on account of age, sex or creed: all were killed from the young and up and a river of blood flowed through this pitiable and unhappy city.*"[xv]

While the sack of this Christian city helped Alp Arslan to promote himself as the defender of Islam, he still didn't want a full-scale war with Byzantium. After taking Ani, he turned back east to the Caucasus to suppress some rebellious Turkmen who had rejected Seljuk rule. Having done this, he withdrew back to Baghdad.

## AFSIN'S RAIDS

But even if the Seljuk Sultan didn't want to invade Byzantium, the Turkmen did. Byzantine Armenia was now almost completely in their hands and this meant that in the 1060s, growing numbers of Turkmen, were focused on one thing: raiding and plundering the rich cities of Byzantine Anatolia.

There was one Turkish emir who epitomised this perfectly: called Afsin, he established a base in Armenia at Mount Amanaus and gathered a large war band, probably several thousand strong. He invaded Byzantine Anatolia routinely in 1066 and 1067, taking advantage of the weaknesses in the Byzantine defences. His actions were in direct contravention of Alp Arslan's orders not to provoke the Byzantines into a retaliatory war. Indeed, he was actually under a death sentence from Alp Arslan for his unruly behaviour, which had involved killing one of the Sultan's most trusted commanders. But this did nothing to stop him. In 1067, he routed the demoralised Byzantine border troops near Melitene, *"...the enemy* [the Turks] *who stood on the banks* [of the Euphrates] *kept shooting at the Romans, causing many casualties and forcing them to turn and run. In this flight a large number of Romans fell, while others were taken captive."*[xvi] He and his Turkmen travelled a spectacular distance – hundreds of miles – right into the heartland of the empire, to sack the great city of Caesarea.

As described in the first chapter, the sack of Caesarea was a step too far. It ignited outrage in Constantinople, paving the way for Romanus' elevation to Emperor. The scene was now set for a whole new chapter in the war in the east.

PART II

# The Battle for Byzantium

*Seljuk Turkish shield*

# 5

# THE LAST ROMAN ARMY

Romanus didn't waste time enjoying the luxuries of his new-found power. He left Constantinople as soon as his administrative duties were finished and crossed over the Bosphorus in early March to assemble an army to confront the Turks. He set up his headquarters in Cappadocia, the heart of Byzantine Anatolia and home to his family estates. There he mustered all the troops he could find. The senator who accompanied him on campaign, Michael Attaleiates, described the pathetic condition of these once proud regiments: *"It was something to see the famous units and their commanders now composed of just a few men, and these bent over by poverty and lacking in proper weapons and warhorses."*[xvii]

This description is a far cry from what the Byzantine army looked like a hundred years before. By the 1060s, the eastern army – previously the backbone of Byzantine military power – had effectively shrunk to garrison units defending the main cities, such as Melitene, Manzikert and Theodosiopolis along the Cappadocian/Armenian border and Antioch and Edessa in the south along the Syrian border. Romanus was appalled by this sad state of affairs. He was a member of the Cappadocian military aristocracy that had led the eastern army in the tenth century, when the Emperors Nicephorus Phocas and John Tzimiskes had humbled the Abbasid Caliphate. His rebellion in 1067 had one real objective – to stop the rot and restore the eastern army to its former glory.

Although the task must have seemed almost impossible, there was one hope. The Byzantine army had always been divided between east and west, and in the west there still existed a reduced, but fairly effective army. This had always been loyal to the reigning Emperor and therefore had survived better than its eastern cousin, which was dominated by the rebellious Cappadocian aristocracy. It was also badly needed to contain the barbarian attacks in the west in the 1040s–60s by the Pechenegs and Oghuz Turks. The western army retained much of the old military structure, containing the last remaining elite cavalry regiments, the Scholae and Excubitors, as well as local levies from Thrace and Greece. Importantly for Romanus, it was also particularly loyal to him since he had been one of its most popular generals, and its soldiers even swore an oath to obey him when he was made Emperor.[xviii]

## THE REVIVAL OF THE EASTERN ARMY

Romanus' aim was to revive the eastern army by using the western army as recruiting sergeants and instructors. To help him do this, he took the western army out of the Balkans. He instructed its commanders to find peaceful solutions to the conflicts on the empire's western borders, along the Danube and in Italy. He left as few troops as possible in the west, and sent almost no reinforcements to help the hard-pressed army holding out in Italy against the Normans.

In early 1068, he set about recruiting young men from the countryside and cities in the east, offering them good pay and equipment. He put experienced soldiers from the western army in command of these raw recruits, carefully choosing suitable commanders. The whole process took several months, so that he wasn't ready to move the new army until around May. But by then he had put together a large army, probably about 20,000 strong.[xix] This army was one of the largest that Byzantium had fielded in the eleventh century. The last time a similar-sized force had gone on the offensive was in the 1030s, when the able general, George Maniaces, had captured Edessa in Syria and parts of Sicily before being recalled by a jealous Emperor.

The bulk of the army was the newly trained Cappadocian regiments, which were ethnically Greek. The elite troops were the cavalry. Consisting of the sons of the Cappadocian and other Anatolian landowners and magnates, they came from wealthy families, rich enough to afford good quality armour and horses. Although the armour wasn't as formidable as that worn by the cataphracts a century ago, they were equipped with either chain-mail tunics or a sleeveless cuirass, usually of scale armour. They wore iron helmets and carried shields, either oval or kite-shaped,[18] and carried lances, swords and maces.

Most of the soldiers were infantry. Armenian infantry are mentioned frequently in Byzantine sources and constituted an important part of Romanus' army. They were tough soldiers, survivors of the genocidal warfare in Armenia with the Turks, and Romanus would use them repeatedly as storm troopers in sieges to batter the enemy gates down. The rest of the infantry

---

18    The kite-shaped shield beloved of the Normans was probably copied from the Byzantines.

were peasants from Cappadocia and the other Anatolian themes, organised into heavy and light infantry. The heavy infantry wore thick padded or quilted garments and thick caps made of felt, and carried large round or kite-shaped shields with spears, swords, axes and iron maces. Although they didn't have the heavy armour of their distant cousins – the Roman legionaries – they were still well drilled and trained.

Light infantry principally consisted of archers armed with composite or compound bows copied from the Huns in the fourth century. Mounted archery skills had disappeared in the Byzantine army by the eleventh century but the infantry archers were still a force to be reckoned with. The Byzantine bows were sophisticated weapons with a flight range estimated at 300 metres, although the 'killing range' would have been less.[xx] There were also javelin throwers and slingers who were used for skirmishing as well as supporting the heavy infantry and archers.

The army was organised into units directly descended from those of the Roman legions.[xxi] This had evolved over the centuries so that by the eleventh century the main operational unit was the *bandum* which probably consisted of 200 men. Units of 1,000 soldiers were called a *drungus*, although by the eleventh century such large units had almost ceased to exist. However, Romanus may have reintroduced them given the large size of the army he created. Also directly descended from the Roman legions was a culture of discipline and training that had been eroded in the eleventh century but is still visible in the records of Romanus' campaigns. Most conspicuous of these was the building of extensive military camps when the army was on campaign. This was very rare for any army to do in the Middle Ages, but for the Byzantines the Roman dedication to building palisades behind moats to protect their camps had survived as a core requirement for an army on the march, and there is no doubt that this practice survived into Romanus' reign.

Although Romanus' aim was to revive the regular Greek regiments of the eastern army, he still employed reasonably large numbers of mercenaries in his army. A unit of Varangians is mentioned fighting in the first Syrian campaign, although most of them were probably left in Constantinople to guard the capital. Norman cavalry are mentioned in Romanus' future campaigns, if not the first one in 1068. He also used as light cavalry the close cousins of the Seljuk Turks – the Pechenegs and Oghuz Turks.

In the spring of 1068, Romanus led his new army out of Cappadocia towards Armenia to give battle to the Sultan. Romanus had many supporters, especially in the eastern provinces. In Cappadocia itself he was a local hero, and the families of the magnates and great landowners regarded him as their saviour. His new regiments would have inspired pride in the faces of the cheering onlookers. Row after row of fresh-faced young men riding their warhorses, the light glinting off newly forged iron swords and freshly painted shields. Their families cheering them on. Parents proud but worried. Excited sisters with jealous younger brothers. Banners and pennants blowing in the wind, many dating back to the regiments of old, they marched east in their thousands. They were, in effect, the last descendants of the Roman legions.

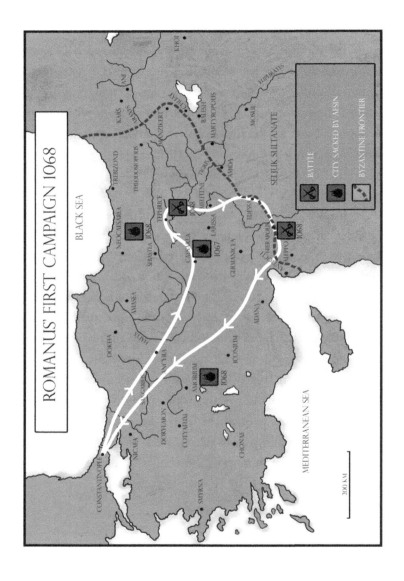

# 6

# THE SYRIAN CAMPAIGN

As Romanus' army marched east in the spring of 1068, surprising news reached them. The expected Turkish onslaught had not materialised. Alp Arslan had in fact withdrawn his army back to Iraq. Although this wasn't clear to the Byzantines, his objective was not invading Byzantium but rather wresting Fatimid control from Syria. The true purpose of his advance into Armenia had been to stamp his authority over the rebellious Turkmen and he had no wish to provoke a full-scale war with the Byzantines.

## ROMANUS ATTACKS SYRIA

While Romanus was pleasantly surprised by this news, nevertheless, having spent three months rebuilding the eastern army, he was keen to test his raw recruits. So, instead of marching east, he turned south to the Byzantine/Arab border in Syria where there was still plenty of fighting with Turkish mercenaries serving the Arab emirates in Aleppo and Hierapolis, which had been putting growing pressure on the key Byzantine strongholds at Antioch and Edessa. In addition,

Romanus was no doubt influenced by the fact that the Syrian frontier had been the traditional battleground between the Byzantines and the Arabs in the past, and was a place where many legendary Byzantine generals, like Nicephorus Phokas, had won their spurs.

But as he was marching south, disaster struck. The Turkish threat from the east had not disappeared. A Turkish war band under the command of the notorious renegade warlord, Afsin, had passed unnoticed through the eastern frontier and sacked another Anatolian city, Neocaesarea, not far from the city of Caesarea, itself sacked by Afsin the year before. Romanus was shocked. He had been wrong-footed. He quickly turned his army around and marched back towards the Armenian frontier. Determined to hunt the Turks down, he immediately took his Cappadocian cavalry and rode into the hills near Tephrike (modern Divrigi in eastern Turkey) in pursuit of Afsin. Meanwhile he sent the rest of the army to Sebasteia to guard against any further Turkmen incursions.

For eight days, Romanus pursued a Turkish war band which he thought was Afsin's. Riding day and night through the mountains, he caught up with them. His Cappadocian cavalry, thirsty for revenge, cornered the Turks and massacred them. All the prisoners were put to the sword. The Turkish plunder was recovered and their prisoners freed.

But they soon discovered that the war band was not Afsin's. It was a smaller group that had been plundering on a lesser scale. Afsin had slipped back to Armenia undisturbed. Even so, Romanus had demonstrated his determination to confront the enemy, and the Turks seem to have been cowed by the presence of the Emperor. For the time being their raids stopped.

Romanus only spent a few days at Sebasteia before resuming his march south. He left a strong force, including Frankish mercenaries, in the border fortress city of Melitene, to guard the eastern frontier, hoping that this force would be sufficient to intercept any further Turkish raids. Then, he led the army south to Syria. En route there was more fighting with Turkish raiders. Grain convoys to feed the troops were attacked. Romanus acted swiftly and drove off the attackers. The army eventually arrived in northern Syria near to Aleppo – a powerful Fatimid Arab emirate.

It may seem strange that Romanus chose to attack the Fatimids when they were enemies of the Seljuks but it should be remembered that, while the Fatimids and Seljuks were nominally at war with each other, the fragmented nature of both of their empires meant that local politics often overrode wider considerations, and the emir of Aleppo was quite happy to employ Seljuk Turkmen as mercenaries led by one of the Seljuk princes, Ibn Khan al-Turkumani. He had been using these to raid Byzantine territory up to the walls of the great city of Antioch.

## THE CAPTURE OF HIERAPOLIS AND THE DEFEAT OF THE EMIR OF ALEPPO

Romanus' swift advance into Syria caught the Arabs by surprise. Pecheneg mercenaries sent on foraging expeditions returned with abundant plunder, including both animals and humans. The army marched on towards Hierapolis, a well-fortified Arab town owing allegiance to the Fatimid emir of Aleppo. Romanus pitched camp beside it.

Meanwhile, an army sent by the emir of Aleppo, containing Bedouin tribesmen and boosted with Turkmen mercenaries, followed in the Byzantines' wake. The Bedouin cavalry had a fearsome reputation with exceptionally fast horses – even faster than those of the Turks – enabling them to make lightning attacks on their enemy. Knowing that he might be caught between the Aleppan army and the Arabs in Hierapolis, he decided to take Hierapolis quickly and immediately launched an assault on the city, using the Varangians and Armenian infantry to batter their way in. After fierce fighting, they were able to force the gates and enter the city. Many of the Arabs had fled earlier, leaving those that remained holding out in a few towers and the citadel. One by one, Romanus stormed the towers, using catapults. He surrounded the citadel and started to build a ramp with earth in front of its walls. At the sight of this, the remaining Arabs offered to pay a ransom in return for their lives. Romanus accepted this and, honouring his pledge, he made sure that they left the city unharmed.

But while Romanus' soldiers were fighting in the town, the Aleppan army was massing outside. It was now a substantial size, maybe 20,000 strong, with Turkmen, Bedouin tribesmen and Mamluk regiments. The Mamluk soldiers were the elite of the Arab armies in the Middle East. Although officially slaves, they were actually exceptionally well paid and highly valued. Mamluks were often Turkish but could also be Arab and sometimes even Armenian or Greek. They were typically bought as boys and trained to fight and ride so that they became professional soldiers.

The Aleppans launched an attack just as Romanus was assaulting the last tower in Hierapolis. Advancing right up to the Byzantine encampment, which was well fortified with a trench and palisade in the ancient Roman style, the Mamluks encountered two elite Byzantine regiments from the western army – the Stratelatai and Scholai. These regiments were supposedly the best in the Byzantine army but the Mamluks drove them back into the camp, killing many of them, capturing some of their standards and taking prisoners who were promptly beheaded, with their severed heads sent to Aleppo.

Romanus was furious when he heard of the western army's pitiful performance. Quickly leading a unit of his newly trained Cappadocian troops out of the camp, he formed a battle line to face the Arabs. The sight of the disciplined Byzantine troops persuaded the Arabs to pull back. Nevertheless, Romanus was deeply worried by the poor performance of the western troops.

With the Aleppan army a stone's throw away, the Byzantines hardly slept that night. It looked as if Romanus' strategy to test his new army in Syria might prove his undoing. He needed to secure a victory the next day if his army was not to be trapped in Hierapolis. But Romanus had years of experience fighting in the Balkans. He spent the night in his tent devising a battle plan.

At dawn, just as Bedouin tribesmen were advancing on the Byzantine camp, Romanus launched a brilliant surprise attack. Without sounding the customary trumpets and bugles, he led his most loyal soldiers – the Cappadocians and Armenians – straight out to meet the Arabs. The ruse worked well. The attacking Bedouin were caught by surprise and pushed back with heavy casualties. The rest of the Byzantine army charged out in support. The Arabs hadn't expected such a determined attack and retreated in chaos.

A Byzantine senator has left us with a vivid description of the battle. He claims that the Byzantines could have completely routed the Aleppan army as it started to flee, especially as the fast Bedouin horses tired more quickly than those of the Byzantines: *"…for although the Arab horses can run very swiftly for a time, they do not bear up well over a long distance.*"[xxii] He thought that the victory should have been followed up with an assault on Aleppo itself. But Romanus was more cautious. For whatever reason, he didn't pursue the retreating enemy. Maybe he feared an ambush. Nevertheless, Romanus had secured an important victory. With the Arabs fleeing back to Aleppo, he stayed at Hierapolis to organise its defence, giving the governorship to an Armenian called Pharasmanios Apokapes. Romanus' capture of Hierapolis was the most important Byzantine victory since the capture of Edessa in 1034.

## ROMANUS' ARMY RETURNS HOME

By now it was late November and winter was on its way. The campaigning season was effectively over. In early December, he marched the army out of Hierapolis towards Aleppo and reached the Arab-held fortress of Azas. He considered attacking it but ultimately decided that its fortifications were too strong. The army continued its march west towards Antioch. There was some skirmishing with the Aleppans en route and Romanus seized the town of Artach, lying midway between Antioch and Aleppo, and recently captured by the Aleppans who used it as a base for attacks on Antioch. A garrison and a commander were installed, making another useful addition to Byzantine defences in Cilicia. Romanus decided not to march to Antioch, the second city in the empire and the centre of its defences in Syria, since it was suffering from a grain shortage and his army would only have imposed an extra burden on it. Besides, the city had no need of help, protected as it was by huge ancient walls and well garrisoned.

Romanus decided to return home. According to the Senator, Attaleiates, the campaign marked a turning point in Byzantine history: "*It was, therefore, during the reign of this emperor* [Romanus] *that the Romans* [Byzantines] *began to stand up to their enemies, recover their more noble outlook and organise their resistance.*"[xxiii] But the march home would be no easy task since the army now faced the difficult ordeal of crossing the Taurus mountain range in midwinter. To begin with, it followed the coast road north from Antioch to a town called Alexandron where the troops started to make their way up into the towering mountain range along tortuous clifftop roads. The change in temperature from the milder winter climate in Syria to the freezing conditions in the mountains started to take its toll on the troops: "*...the men marching with him... suddenly found themselves in icy cold weather, with everything covered in frost... Thus it happened that horses, mules and men, especially those whose bodies were not robust or well clothed, froze to death in the sudden cold and had to be left on the road, a pitiable sight.*"[xxiv]

The senator, Attaleiates, vividly described his own narrow escape from death on one of the cliff-top routes. His horse was suffering from some form of colitis which caused it to stop and bend its forelegs sufficiently for Attaleiates to slide off, before it fell headlong down a precipice: "*As I got the horse to stand again by forcing him with the reins, he immediately lurched uncontrollably on his own and threw himself over the cliff. But I remained safe and praised God for rescuing me from the danger.*"[xxv]

Fortunately for posterity, Attaleiates survived,[19] and the army's morale improved as it finally passed through the Taurus

---

19    Michael Attaleiates is the main source for Romanus' reign. Without his chronicle, little would be known about it.

Mountains into the more clement lands of southern Anatolia. But there they found news of a cruel and utterly unexpected blow. The renegade Turkish warlord, Afsin, had struck again.

## AFSIN'S SACK OF AMORIUM

Afsin epitomised the lawless and independent spirit of the Turkmen. His raids into Byzantium were not only condemned by Alp Arslan, but he was actually under a death sentence for killing one of his favourite courtiers. Nevertheless, this seems only to have encouraged him to make ever more daring raids. While Romanus was fighting in Syria, he had struck again. The problem was that the strong garrison Romanus had left in Melitene had done nothing to stop him. These troops should have intercepted him but their commander just sat behind the walls and let the Turks pass into the interior. Maybe this commander (we don't know his name) was a traitor or simply a coward. Whatever the case, Romanus learned to his cost that he'd appointed the wrong person. Afsin's warriors rode unhindered west into the heartland of the empire.

And this time they rode astonishingly deep into Byzantine territory. Travelling over 300 miles west past Melitene, they reached another major Byzantine city called Amorium. Just like Caesarea, the city didn't expect Turkish nomads to come anywhere near its walls. Attaleiates says that Afsin took it by storm, massacred most of the population and carried the rest away as slaves. There was nothing that Romanus could do. By the time he received news of the raid, Afsin was already well on his way back to Seljuk Armenia. It was a huge blow to Romanus' prestige. And it was especially galling after his successful Syrian campaign.

It was a long march for Romanus and his army back to Constantinople in the depths of winter. He only reached the city close to the end of January. Leaving the new Anatolian regiments in the provinces, and assigning the western troops and the mercenaries to winter quarters outside the city, he reached the Bosphorus.

Looking across the water, Romanus and his troops would probably have seen snow covering the great dome of Hagia Sophia, visible for miles around the city. As they filed into boats to cross over to the holy city, Romanus must have cursed Afsin. He knew the Doukai would do everything in their power to use this tragedy to discredit him. The sack of Amorium hung like a black cloud over his return, as dark and threatening as the winter sky.

# 7

# NORMANS AND TURKS

In spite of Afsin's sack of Amorium, Romanus organised a triumphal march through the city's Golden Gate to celebrate his victory in Syria.[20] It was the first for decades. Triumphal marches were an important sign of military success, and the absence of one for so long was testimony to the decline of the Byzantine army. Although the sack of Amorium had damaged his credibility, Romanus was still in a strong position. He had the support of most of the nobility, in particular the powerful Comneni family, the main rivals to the Doukai. The Empress had also just given birth to their first child – a boy called Nicephorus – which further reinforced Romanus' claim to the throne since any child 'born in the purple'[21] had a claim to the imperial throne, in Byzantine eyes.

Nevertheless, Amorium's destruction made it clearer than ever that to retain his popularity, Romanus had to secure a decisive victory over the Turks. Therefore, in January 1069, he reverted back to his original plan of the previous year for an offensive into the East with the aim of securing the

---

20  The heavily fortified entrance to the city walls that can still be seen in modern Istanbul.

21  The Greek word 'Porphyrogenitus' means 'born in the purple'.

eastern frontier around Manzikert. After he'd distributed in customary fashion the salaries and honours to the senators and military commanders,[22] he crossed over the Bosphorus from Constantinople to muster the army. The same as in the previous year, he took the western army to augment his new eastern regiments.

## THE NORMAN REBELLION

But as he was waiting for the eastern army to assemble, he heard some surprising news. The largest group of Norman mercenaries in Byzantine pay, led by a man called Robert Crispin, had rebelled. Stationed on the Armenian frontier in the fortress Maurokastro, midway between Theodosiopolis and Manzikert, this unit of Normans, probably about 500 strong, felt they had been underpaid by Romanus and had started to rob the Byzantine tax collectors. Romanus wanted to put an end to this insurrection quickly. He disliked the mercenary troops anyway which was in reality the source of the Normans' complaints.

Romanus was still based just across the Bosphorus from Constantinople, too far away to lead his troops personally against Crispin. So, he ordered five regiments of the western army, stationed close to the Normans on the Armenian border, to put the rebellion down. These Byzantine soldiers were under the command of a general called Samuel Alousianos. On 12 April 1069, which was Easter Day, and the most important day in the medieval Christian calendar,[23] Alousianos attacked.

---

22  A centuries-old ceremony during which bags of golden coins were literally handed by the Emperor to the great and the good.

23  Easter was much more widely celebrated than Christmas in the Middle Ages.

The result was a shambles. It was meant to be a surprise attack with Easter Day chosen since the Normans would be distracted with the Christian festivities. The soldiers from the western army crept up on the Norman camp which was not defended with a palisade or ditch. But the Byzantine sources say they tripped over the tent ropes as they approached. More likely is that they failed to see the tripwires hung with bells on them placed around the camp, a tactic widely used by medieval armies. Whatever the truth, the Normans quickly picked up their weapons and drove the Byzantines out of their camp, killing quite a number, and afterwards pursuing them on horseback.

Crispin didn't want to provoke too strong a response from Romanus, so he released the prisoners and cared for the Byzantine wounded. Nevertheless, Romanus was still furious. He led his army to Dorylaion, the main Byzantine military hub in Anatolia, equipped with a huge arsenal and barracks. There, envoys arrived from Crispin, pleading for clemency on the basis that they had been attacked by surprise, and sacrilegiously on Easter Day itself. Attaleiates reports that at first Romanus was willing to listen to their claims, and when Crispin himself arrived, he swore his loyalty to Romanus. But other soldiers in Romanus' army, including a prominent German mercenary, denounced Crispin and persuaded Romanus to arrest him. Romanus may have made a mistake for, in spite of his disobedience, Crispin was a good soldier, and his arrest made him into a personal enemy.[24]

More immediately, Crispin's arrest didn't even solve the problems with the rebellious Normans. With Crispin sent to a prison at Abydos on the Bosphorus, the rest of the Normans

---

24    This was to have unfortunate consequences for Romanus later in his reign.

openly revolted. They stayed in the Armenian theme, in the fortress at Maurokastro, and continued to take the law into their own hands. Romanus left them there. At least they presented an obstacle to the Turks. Returning to his original plan, he marched his army from Dorylaion to what was left of the city of Caesarea, so badly sacked by Afsin in 1067. He had amassed a large army by the time he arrived, boosted by the incoming regiments of Cappadocian and other Anatolian soldiers. Nevertheless, a worrying aspect of the Crispin incident was the poor performance of the regular Byzantine soldiers in the western army against Crispin's Normans, since it showed that there was still a long way to go before the Byzantine soldiers could match the Normans.

## ROMANUS DEFEATS A TURKISH RAIDING PARTY

After this distraction, Romanus was ready to embark on his march to Armenia. He led the army from Caesarea east to the town of Larissa, where a large Turkish raiding party was nearby. Romanus sent out scouts and there was some skirmishing with the Turks which persuaded him to advance with the whole army to meet them in battle. The Byzantines marched into a plain to find themselves surrounded by the Turks occupying the hills.

As he had done in Syria, Romanus led his army with skill and inspired his troops to fight well. The Turks charged down from the hills, hoping to catch the Byzantines before they could form into battle lines. But Romanus was ready for them. He kept discipline in the Byzantine ranks. There was a good performance by the new eastern army, in particular a regiment from Lykonia,[xxvi] the province next to Cappadocia.

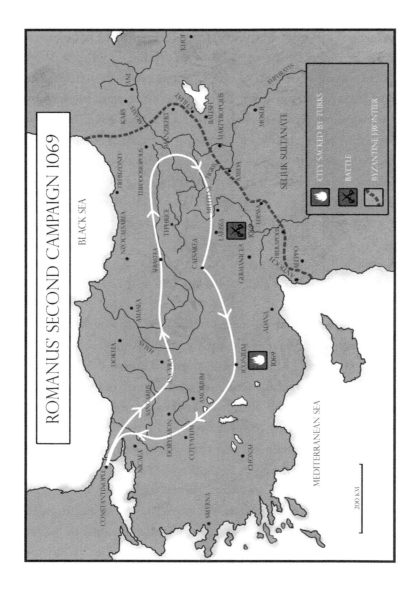

ROMANUS' SECOND CAMPAIGN 1069

This regiment, together with another from the western army, charged the Turks head on and put them to flight. The whole army advanced into the hills and the Turks fell back in headlong retreat.

Romanus sent the light Pecheneg cavalry ahead to try and cut off the Turks' retreat as the slower Byzantine infantry marched forward. Nevertheless, most of the Turks got away. Romanus pursued them down the valley where they had come from, keeping his troops in tight formation, and waiting for the ambush that he knew would be inevitable.

But the Turks had a different plan. Instead of trying to ambush the advancing rows of Byzantine infantry, Turkish horsemen wheeled across the hills to attack the Byzantine camp from behind. What they didn't know was that Romanus had expected this and left it well defended, with a group of Norman soldiers (a different band from Crispin's) and several Byzantine units. There was a fierce fight. The Turks, hoping for easy pickings, found themselves confronted by Norman and Byzantine swords. The Normans fought better than the Byzantines and were mainly responsible for driving the Turks off.[xxvii] When Romanus heard of the attack on the camp, he called off the main army's advance. It was late afternoon and the soldiers were tired after a day's fighting. Although most of the Turks had got away, it was still a victory.

The next day, Romanus took revenge on the Turkish prisoners. He executed every single one, numbering about a hundred. One of them, who claimed to be their leader, promised a large ransom as well as the release of Byzantine prisoners if he was spared. But Romanus wasn't in the mood for negotiation. With the memory of the humiliating sack of Amorium no doubt fresh in his mind, he had the protesting Turk beheaded in front of him.[xxviii]

The rest of the campaign is poorly supported by contemporary sources. Indeed, the only detailed description of it is that recorded by the Byzantine senator, Michael Attaleiates. According to him, Romanus decided to call off the whole campaign, thinking that the Turks were in retreat back to Armenia, and that it would be best to rest the army for a more decisive campaign the following year, but he was persuaded by Attaleiates (who records this indulging in uncharacteristic self-promotion) to continue the campaign with a march to Armenia.[xxix]

Romanus resumed the campaign, marching the army past Melitene and crossing the Euphrates. It advanced quite far east, within a hundred miles of Manzikert and Chilat, before Romanus again decided to stop. Again Attaleiates claims this was a mistake. The reason is not entirely clear but it seems that Romanus was ill, for Attaleiates says that he needed to go north in search of *"snow and cold water, for which he felt an uncontrollable need since his body had greatly overheated"*.[xxx] Leaving the bulk of the army under the command of a loyal general called Philaretus Brachamius,[25] Romanus rode north-west with a smaller group of troops into the cooler climate of the Taurus Mountains. There he rested and seems to have recovered his health. But he'd made an uncharacteristic tactical mistake as soon became clear.

## THE TURKS SACK ICONIUM

Romanus had again underestimated the competence of the troops he'd left guarding the frontier. When a new and

---

25   Although Philaretus was loyal to Romanus, and after his death, revolted against the Doukai and seized Antioch, he was reviled by the Byzantines because in the 1080s he converted to Islam.

particularly resourceful Turkish war band appeared, they defeated Philaretus' forces who fled to join the Emperor. Although this time the Turks weren't commanded by Afsin, the infamous Turkish warlord who had sacked Amorium, their leader must have been a very daring chieftain for he led his raiding party several hundred miles behind the front line into the heartland of the empire.

Romanus had been outwitted. His slower-moving troops simply couldn't match the speed of the Turks. It was like being trapped in a revolving door. He immediately marched after them but by then it was too late. Then he received devastating news. The city of Iconium had been sacked. It was a large, rich city in the Anatolikon theme, in the west of Anatolia, so far behind the front line that its inhabitants were not expecting an attack and the city's defences were easily overcome. Exactly as the sack of Amorium had been the year before, it was another devastating blow to his prestige.

In desperation, Romanus hoped to minimise the disgrace by catching the retreating Turks. He nearly managed it. He sent messengers to the governor of Antioch, Chatatourios, who was a loyal ally of his, instructing him to block the Turks from getting back into Syria. It looked as if Chatatourios would succeed. Blocked by Romanus' army in the north, the Turks' only escape route was to the south through the difficult Taurus Mountains and down to the Mediterranean coastline, where Chatatourios was waiting for them.

Romanus sent orders to Armenian troops garrisoning the mountaintops to intercept the Turks. They did a good job peppering the Turks with spears and arrows and causing them to abandon most of their booty. But the Armenians couldn't stop them and most of the Turks managed to get through the mountains and down to the coast.

In the Cilician Plain, Chatatourios tried to intercept the Turks at a place called Mopsouestia, near to the coast. But somehow they managed to give him the slip. Making use of their excellent horsemanship, they deftly skirted around the Byzantine stronghold at Antioch to find safety in Syria.

The sack of Iconium was another devastating blow for Romanus. For a second time he had failed to protect the interior of the empire from Turkish raids. It was now autumn and he had no choice but to return to Constantinople. There was to be no triumphal march on his return this time. Instead, he returned to the great city to find that his deadly enemies – the Doukai – were stirring up discontent like the furies in a Greek tragedy.

# 8

# WAR AND PEACE

The year 1070 was the only one in Romanus' reign when he did not lead his army into battle. Michael Attaleiates ominously recounts that: *"From this time on, the empire of the Romans was beset with adversities and difficulties."*[xxxi] But the story of this year was more intriguing than that. It was not only the prelude to the great Byzantine offensive in 1071 that would culminate in the pivotal Battle of Manzikert, but it was also a year that would contain plenty of bizarre twists and surprises.

Although detailed source material for this year is severely lacking, we can conjecture that there were probably several reasons behind Romanus' decision to stay in Constantinople. One of them was almost certainly a political crisis stemming from his failure to prevent the sacking of Iconium and Amorium. Relations with the Doukai seem to have reached breaking point. We know from one Byzantine source[xxxii] that Romanus actually arrested Caesar John and considered putting him to death but finally decided to settle with taking oaths of loyalty from him and his sons. Caesar John was exiled to his estates in Bithynia where he remained until after the Battle of Manzikert. Other than that, there is frustratingly little else that we know about the tensions between the Doukai and Romanus, but we can be fairly sure that there was a political crisis in the capital, maybe even an attempted coup against Romanus by the Doukai, as alluded to by a Byzantine source written nearly a century later: *"If it lay within their* [the Doukai] *power, they would have chosen that he not even live, for he was an annoyance to them, and they hated him as a noble and brave man."*[xxxiii]

Another important reason is that Romanus almost certainly wanted to concentrate on building up the army he took to Manzikert the following year in 1071. Both Byzantine and Arab sources are unanimous that the size of the army fielded in 1071 was much larger than those in his previous campaigns. Mustering such a force would have taken time, and Romanus must have been busy in 1070, recruiting and training the eastern regiments who he wanted to be the backbone of his army, as well as hiring mercenaries.

A further reason is also the biggest surprise of all – there was apparently an offer of a truce by the Seljuk Sultan, Alp Arslan, in 1070. While this is not mentioned by any of the Byzantine sources, both of the main Arab authors for this period, Bar Hebraeus and Sibt Ibn al-Jawzi,[xxxiv] state unequivocally that such a truce was made. Although their histories are far briefer than that of Attaleiates and written over a hundred years later, they are otherwise reliable and the conclusion must be that a truce was agreed.

Why did Alp Arslan want a truce? This is not as surprising as it might at first seem since Seljuk ambitions, as described earlier, lay with extending their dominion over the Fatimids, not the Byzantines. In addition, Seljuk encouragement to the Turkmen to raid Byzantine Anatolia in the 1060s had started to give the Turkmen too much autonomy. Therefore, in 1070 a truce with the Byzantines satisfied a number of Seljuk aims: it prevented a Byzantine attack; gave them more authority over the Turkmen; and it allowed Alp Arslan to concentrate on a war against the Fatimids in Syria.

## MANUEL COMNENUS AND THE NAWAKIYYA

Returning to the Byzantine side of events, with the truce in place, Romanus stayed in Constantinople and sent Manuel Comnenus with an army to guard the eastern frontier. His choice of a member of the Comneni was politically significant since they were the main rival to the Doukai, and by giving them such a senior position he hoped to keep the Doukai in check.

Since there was a truce with the Sultan, Manuel was under instructions just to monitor the eastern frontier. But the reality was that rogue Turkmen war bands were happily ignoring the truce and raiding Byzantine territory. To the south, Hierapolis, captured by Romanus in 1068, was also under pressure from the Fatimid emir of Aleppo.

At first, Manuel had some success against some Turkish war bands raiding into Byzantine territory. Michael Attaleiates hints that Romanus was even slightly jealous of his success,[xxxv] and it is possible that personal pride might have influenced his decision to order half of Manuel's army to head south to reinforce Hierapolis – the trophy city captured in Romanus' 1068 campaign – which was under pressure from the Arabs. Whatever the reasons, this weakened Manuel's forces just at the moment when he came face to face with a more formidable Turkish war band – that of the Nawakiyya. But this was no ordinary war band. It was under the command of Erbasghan,

Alp Arslan's brother-in-law who had rebelled against the Sultan and was acting in open defiance of his orders.

Who exactly were the Nawakiyya?[xxxvi] Although early Seljuk records are almost non-existent, we know that they were a large Turkmen grouping that started to settle in Syria along the Byzantine frontier around the beginning of Alp Arslan's reign in 1063. After fighting as mercenaries for the Fatimid emirs, like the emir of Aleppo (it is quite likely that they fought against Romanus in his first campaign in Syria in 1068), they decided to invade Byzantine territory in 1070 on their own.

But the bizarre twist that now took hold of Byzantine-Seljuk relations stemmed from Alp Arslan's fear of the Nawakiyya. Since they were aristocratic, and indeed related to the Seljuks themselves, they posed a real threat as contenders for leadership of the Turkmen. This would now lead to an astonishing twist in Byzantine-Seljuk relations.

Erbasghan had led his war band to near Sebasteia when Manuel attacked him. Manuel seems to have been winning the battle until the Turks performed their favourite tactic of a feigned retreat, whereupon Manuel's soldiers fell straight into the trap. They pursued the Turks, breaking up their own ranks, only to find that the hunter swiftly became the hunted as the Turks surrounded them and charged home with their sabres. Manuel's forces were slaughtered or surrendered, their camp was seized, and the survivors fled to the safety of Sebasteia's walls.

Erbasghan even took Manuel prisoner. Then, he sprang the biggest surprise of all. Instead of torturing him or even asking for a ransom, he set out for Constantinople with an offer of peace. He explained that he had been outlawed by the Sultan and wanted to join the Byzantines to fight against

Alp Arslan. This extraordinary turnaround was welcomed by
Romanus, who met him with Manuel in tow, and honoured
him with the rank of Proedros,[26] to the surprise of Attaleiates
who described the Turkish leader as: *almost a pygmy in height,
and his face was that of a Skythian* [Byzantine generic term for
the Asiatic nomads] *and ugly because this people are of Skythian
ancestry and have inherited their depravity and deformity.*[xxxvii] In
spite of this, disappointingly for Romanus, it seems that few
of Erbasghan's followers stayed with him.

Romanus' welcome of Erbasghan had unexpected
consequences. It alarmed Alp Arslan, who tore up the
truce and immediately despatched his most formidable, if
uncontrollable, commander to invade Byzantine territory
– the redoubtable Afsin who had sacked Caesarea in 1067,
and both Neocaesarea and Amorium in 1068. Returning
to do what he was best at, and this time with the Sultan's
blessing, Afsin threatened to lay waste another Byzantine
city if Erbasghan was not handed over. When this was not
forthcoming, he galloped deep into Byzantine territory to fulfil
his threat, bypassing the Byzantine cities in central Anatolia,
which were probably by now better defended, and finding a
city called Chonae in the south-west of Anatolia.

Chonae was another wealthy Byzantine city similar to
Afsin's other victims, and not expecting to be attacked since
it was so deep in Byzantine territory. It was famous for having
a great church dedicated to the Archangel Michael, richly
decorated with the finest mosaics which attracted pilgrims from
a wide area. In spite of having a fortress on a mountainside, its
inhabitants appear to have been taken completely by surprise.
Instead of going to the fortress, many of them fled to an

---

26   A Byzantine term for an honorary senator.

ancient underground cistern where fresh water was siphoned off from a nearby river. But this did not save them. As the Turks were defiling the great church and slaughtering anyone still above ground, the unlucky citizens were victims of a flash flood in the cistern from the river following a heavy rainstorm. Horrified, they were sucked down by the torrent of water, and their drowned bodies later disgorged.

The news that yet another great city had been destroyed by the Turks unnerved the people of Constantinople. From now on, God's displeasure with his chosen people became the only explanation for the empire's grotesque misfortunes, as Attaleiates wrote: "*...it was as though these disasters were being caused by divine anger.*"[xxxviii]

Back in the Great Palace, Romanus was exasperated by this turn of events. He wanted to pursue Afsin immediately. He was "*chafing to cross over* [the Bosphorus] *with the soldiers he had with him, and do all he could to aid those in the east.*"[xxxix] But reluctantly he stayed in the palace. Yet he had not been idle. He had spent the year preparing for a great offensive the following spring. In spite of the success of Erbasghan's and Afsin's raids, and the casualties suffered by Manuel Comnenus' army, the Byzantine army was now the largest it had been for more than a century. It would soon be ready to march east for the most critical campaign yet.

# 9

# THE MARCH TO
# MANZIKERT

In late 1070, yet more bad news reached Constantinople.
With the truce broken, the Seljuk Sultan himself, Alp
Arslan, had invaded Byzantine Armenia and taken the key
frontier fortress of Manzikert. Ironically, the threat of a major
Seljuk invasion played into Romanus' hands. There was panic
in the capital, just as there had been in 1067. For Romanus this
was his last chance. Popular support for him had dwindled as
the Turkish raids continued. Relations with the Doukai had
reached breaking point. Caesar John, exiled to his estates in
Bithynia, was waiting like a snake in the grass to strike back.
To survive, Romanus needed a decisive victory over the Turks.
And his first objective would be Manzikert

Not only was the Sultan there but to stop the Turkmen
raids he needed to recapture both Manzikert and the Turkish
stronghold at Chliat. These two fortresses, separated by about
fifty miles, controlled the Turkmen's gateway into Anatolia.
Recent examination[xl] of the routes used by the Turkmen
shows that almost all of them passed through this axis to find
their favourite pasturelands in eastern Anatolia. By securing
control of both fortresses, Romanus could block the Turkish
raiding at its point of origin.

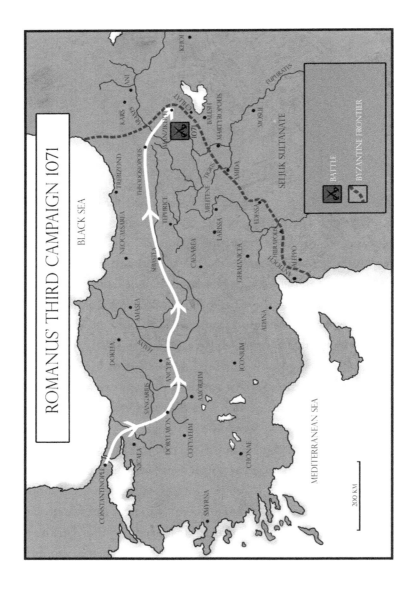

ROMANUS' THIRD CAMPAIGN 1071

BLACK SEA

MEDITERRANEAN SEA

SELJUK SULTANATE

BATTLE

BYZANTINE FRONTIER

200 KM

CONSTANTINOPLE

NICAEA

DORYLAEUM

COTYAEUM

CHONAE

SMYRNA

AMORIUM

ANCYRA

ICONIUM

ADANA

GERMANICIA

CAESAREA

LARISSA

MELITENE

TEPHRICE

SEBASTI

AMASEA

DOKEA

SANGARIUS

HALYS

IRIS

NEOCAESAREA

TREBIZOND

THEODOSIOPOLIS

ARAXES

KARS

ANI

KHOI

MANZIKERT

CHLIAT

ARETES

1071

BALESH

MARTYROPOLIS

TIGRIS

AMIDA

MOSUL

EUPHRATES

EDESSA

HIERAPOLIS

ANTIOCH

ALEPPO

ORONTES

# The Mystery of the Quarrel Between Romanus and Eudocia

Romanus left Constantinople in mid-March. According to Attaleiates,[27] the march east was filled with superstitious portents of doom. These began when Romanus disembarked on the Asiatic side of the Bosphorus at a different place from usual, a town called Helenopolis, which was laughingly referred to by locals as Eleeinopolis or 'the pitiful city', a pun in Greek on its name. When the imperial tent was set up in this unlucky town, its central pole broke, causing the whole tent to collapse. More ominous still was when Romanus advanced into the Anatolikon theme, a fire broke out in the village that he had chosen to stay in, burning many of his horses alive and destroying most of his weapons and equipment.

But Attaleiates' portents of doom should be dismissed as a distraction. Writing years afterwards, he was looking for evidence of divine displeasure to explain the catastrophic defeat that was yet to befall Byzantium. The truth is that the atmosphere at the time was probably just the opposite. While there must have been apprehension, there must also have been great hope. For the Senate and the magnates of the empire had entrusted Romanus with the largest army since the reign of Basil II, and a decisive victory over the Seljuks must have seemed possible.

It is at this point that we should consider a point that has baffled historians for centuries. Why did Romanus take Andronicus Doukas, the son of his main rival, Caesar John, with him on this crucial campaign? As we shall see, this was

---

27  Michael Attaleiates is the only contemporary observer to leave us with a detailed account of Romanus' march east and the subsequent campaign that culminated in the Battle of Manzikert.

to prove catastrophic. However, Attaleiates' commentary may provide some unexpected insight into this subject. This lies with an intriguing description of Romanus' relations with his wife, the Empress Eudocia, as they parted company on the eve of the great campaign.

Attaleiates recounts a serious disagreement between the two of them which caused the Empress to refuse to accompany Romanus when he crossed the Bosphorus. This is all the more surprising since their relationship was apparently a strong one and she had recently borne him two sons in quick succession. Attaleiates says that to patch up their disagreement, Romanus sent her a white dove which had unexpectedly settled in his hands as he was crossing the Bosphorus by boat. When she received the dove, she immediately decided to end their quarrel and rushed to join him. They then spent several happy days together before he marched east.

So, what was their quarrel about? Attaleiates only says that their disagreement was *"a result of certain delicate matters which occur between married couples"*, but it was more likely to have been a disagreement over politics. Not only was Eudocia in love with Romanus but she was also a shrewd political operator herself.

Their disagreement could well have been over the critical issue of Andronicus Doukas. Did Eudocia disagree with Romanus' lenient treatment of him? Did she see more clearly than Romanus the Doukas' capacity for treachery? Did she want Andronicus put under house arrest like his father, Caesar John? Was she angry that her advice was ignored? We will never know the answers to these questions but, as will become clear in the unfolding events of the Manzikert campaign, the Empress may have been more far-sighted than her husband.

## ROMANUS MARCHES EAST

Romanus set off from Constantinople, gathering troops as he went. He crossed the Sangarius River over the Zompos bridge, well known in medieval times but nothing of which survives today. Although he dismissed some of the local troops as not good enough, he still gathered a large army as he went east. In Cappadocia, Romanus was back in his home country. He frequently left the army to visit his estates in the area and stayed at a fortress that he had constructed. He crossed the Halys River and advanced to Caesarea, which had been so savagely attacked in 1067.

While Romanus' army mainly consisted of his new eastern regiments, there were still mercenaries, including Pechenegs and Oghuz Turks from the Balkans, and Franks, Normans and Germans. The unreliability of these troops was shown yet again when a group of Germans was found pillaging the countryside outside Caesarea. Romanus was particularly angry with them, not least since they were apparently part of his own bodyguard.[28] Deeply affronted by the Emperor's punishments, they marched en masse to his tent to protest their case. In a scene reminiscent of the rebellion of the Norman knight, Crispin, Romanus had to call up his regular Byzantine troops to force them to obey his orders. The Germans were dismissed and probably sent to garrison a different part of the empire.

From Caesarea, Romanus marched to Sebasteia. There, they came upon the corpses of Manuel Comnenus' soldiers who had been killed by Erbasghan the previous year, which

---

28  Strangely, the Germans are not mentioned by Byzantine sources in previous campaigns, and Romanus' personal bodyguard was probably mainly made up of his favourite Cappadocian soldiers.

filled the Byzantine troops with apprehension.[xli] However, Romanus encouraged them to be confident that victory could still be theirs. And there were good reasons for this since, unknown to most in his army, Romanus was cleverly tricking Alp Arslan into believing that the Byzantines were not marching to attack Armenia but were in search of peace.

## ROMANUS DECEIVES ALP ARSLAN

The historical records are particularly thin when it comes to Alp Arslan's capture of Manzikert. Indeed, even the exact date is not known but it was probably in late 1070. Quite why the Byzantine garrison surrendered so quickly when Manzikert was able to defeat Alp Arslan's predecessor, Tughril, in 1055, is a mystery. Perhaps they felt that they had no hope of survival against Alp Arslan's main army, especially given that Romanus was at this time nearly 1,000 miles away in Constantinople. Or perhaps they were bribed.

Following the fall of Manzikert, Alp Arslan moved along the Byzantine frontier to the next Byzantine stronghold – the well-fortified city of Edessa. It was there, according to the Arab sources (the Byzantine ones are silent about this) that Romanus sent an envoy to him, proposing a renewal of the previous year's truce, including the swap of Manzikert for Hierapolis. Although Romanus was looking for a decisive victory over the Turks, his peace offer was a clever tactical move since, at the time, he would have still been in Caesarea, a long way from Manzikert, and he wanted to delay Alp Arslan for as long as possible to get his army to Armenia before the Sultan.

According to the Arab sources,[xlii] a truce of some sort was concluded, resulting in Alp Arslan abandoning the siege of

Edessa,[29] and not attacking Hierapolis.[30] Instead, he left the Byzantine frontier and advanced straight to Aleppo, the main Fatimid city in northern Syria, to lay siege to this redoubtable stronghold as a prelude to his conquest of the whole of Fatimid Syria. Romanus' ruse of a peace offer had worked well.

At Aleppo, again according to Arab sources but not Byzantine ones, Alp Arslan received yet another proposal from Romanus, this time from one of his generals called Leo Diabatenus, who demanded that he stop the Turkmen from raiding Byzantium as part of the truce. It is hinted that this demand contained a threat to attack Armenia if he didn't agree. In reality, Romanus' peace offer was working well. It was buying him time to get his army to Manzikert, and the closer he got the harder he could bargain.

But it was at this point that the mist finally lifted from Alp Arslan's eyes and he realised he was being tricked. According to the Arab sources, when he realised this he panicked, ordering an immediate withdrawal from Aleppo back to Armenia to meet the Byzantines in battle. Indeed, his retreat was so precipitous that he only took his Mamluk guard of 4,000 men with him, leaving the local levies behind, and when he crossed the Euphrates, apparently many of his men and horses were drowned in the crossing.

Why was Alp Arslan so alarmed? His panic suggests something more than simple irritation that he'd let himself be tricked by Romanus. A more likely reason is that he knew Erbasghan was now in Romanus' pay.[31] The combination of a Seljuk pretender and a strong Byzantine army was deeply

---

29  The Byzantine garrison at Edessa also put up a much stouter resistance to Alp Arslan than that at Manzikert.

30  Hierapolis had been captured by Romanus in 1068 in his first campaign.

31  Although, rather surprisingly, there is no explicit mention that Erbasghan was part of Romanus' army in the Manzikert campaign.

worrying. The Turkmen were untrustworthy and could easily be persuaded to switch their allegiance to Erbasghan. He had to get to Armenia before Romanus did.

The scene was now set for a decisive showdown between him and Romanus. One of the most important battles of the Middle Ages was about to be fought.

# 10

# THE ARMIES CLASH

J ust as Alp Arslan was retreating from Aleppo, Romanus
reached Theodosiopolis, the largest Byzantine fortress on
the edge of Armenia. With massive walls and a deep moat, it
was a bastion against the Seljuk raiders from the east who had
devastated the region.

There, reinforcements arrived. The Dux of Theodosiopolis,
Nicephorus Basilakes, an ardent supporter of Romanus,
brought troops from Syria and Armenia,[xliii] adding what was
in effect the rest of Byzantium's available Anatolian soldiers to
Romanus' Cappadocian levies. With these, Romanus now had
by far the largest Byzantine army ever assembled in the whole
of the eleventh century. Arab and Armenian sources claim that
it numbered hundreds of thousands, although these numbers
can be dismissed as a gross exaggeration. Byzantine sources
do not give numbers but are clear that it was the largest army
that Romanus had led into battle.[xliv] Most modern estimates[xlv]
put it at around 40,000 soldiers, a very large force for its time,
and probably nearly twice the size of the armies Romanus had
fielded in 1068 and 1069.

The great majority of this army were regular Byzantine
troops. These included the western army, commanded by

its Dux, Nicephorus Bryennius, probably numbering some 5–10,000 men. There were also significant numbers of Armenian infantry, which are frequently mentioned in all of Romanus' campaigns. But the bulk of the army was Romanus' new eastern regiments. Drawn from Cappadocia as well as the themes across Anatolia,[32] they might have numbered some 20–30,000.

Mercenaries were more limited in number. There were some Norman and Frankish cavalry, probably only around 1,000, under the command of Roussel de Bailleul.[33] There was probably a more significant number of Pecheneg and Oghuz Turk mercenaries, say 5,000. No sources mention Varangian regiments being present on this campaign, although some almost certainly were with the Emperor, as we will discuss later.

Then Romanus proceeded to do something which has been the subject of intense controversy ever since: he divided the army in two. Following a council of war with his generals, he rejected a defensive strategy and decided to attack simultaneously the two Seljuk strongholds: Manzikert and Chliat. Michael Attaleiates is at pains to explain that this was a carefully thought-out and sensible strategy, contrary to views expressed by later commentators that it was a major blunder.[34] He emphasises that the division of the army was pragmatic since it was the quickest way of taking both Manzikert and Chliat, before the Sultan Arp Arslan arrived with the main Seljuk army.

Initially, Romanus sent a strong reconnaissance force towards Chliat, consisting of Pechenegs, as well as the

---

32  Aside from Cappadocia, the other principal Anatolian themes were Koloneia, Charsianon, Anatolikon, Pisidia, Lykaonia, Chaldia and Armeniakon.

33  Who was later to become one of Byzantium's most dangerous traitors.

34  Michael Attaleiates was the only eyewitness who wrote a detailed account of the whole campaign.

Frankish mercenaries under Roussel de Bailleul, to scout out the Seljuk stronghold. But, hearing that the Sultan's forces were approaching Chliat, Romanus quickly decided to strengthen his attack on the fortress by sending one of his senior generals, Joseph Trachaneiotes, with further troops. Attaleiates is confusing about the total size of the force that Romanus entrusted to Trachaneiotes since he says that it was *"far more numerous than the soldiers retained by the emperor"*.[xlvi] Many historians have taken this literally to mean that Romanus actually despatched more than half of the army with Trachaneiotes. However, this simply doesn't make sense since we know that at Manzikert, Romanus led the western army and most of the eastern army, together with the Armenian infantry and considerable numbers of Oghuz Turks – i.e. the majority of the troops he had marched east with.

The answer could lie in confusion over the nuances of meaning in the translation from the medieval Greek. When Attaleiates says that the soldiers Trachaneiotes took were more numerous than those retained by the Emperor, the word 'retained' could well refer to Romanus' own personal retinue – i.e. his retainers meaning his own bodyguard – rather than the entire army. This is supported by further comments Attaleiates makes to the effect that Romanus' own bodyguard were seldom used in battle and were therefore available for this special expedition. Indeed, it seems plausible that Romanus gave Trachaneiotes the Varangian Guard, who would have been a key part of his personal retinue, since Attaleiates mentions *"a sizeable body of infantry"* that joined Trachaneiotes, and it is well-known that the Varangians always fought on foot in traditional Viking style. It is also relevant that the Varangians are not mentioned by any source as being present at the Battle of Manzikert, suggesting that they had been sent somewhere else with Chliat the only likely destination. It also shouldn't be forgotten that Romanus greatly preferred Byzantine troops over mercenaries like the Varangians, so their departure would have caused him little grief. Therefore, it seems likely that Trachaneiotes' force included the Varangians, Normans, Pechenegs and some Byzantine troops in a force that was probably some 5,000–10,000 strong, but certainly much smaller than half the army.

The purpose of sending Trachaneiotes to Chliat was to block the Sultan's advance while Romanus took Manzikert. Speed was of the essence because of the news that Alp Arslan's advance guard was already in the area around Chliat. In particular, Romanus was worried about a scorched earth policy that the Seljuks might employ around Chliat which would stop the Byzantines living off the land as they besieged Chliat. Attaleiates is at pains to clarify how important this consideration was: *"Then they* [the Byzantines] *would have to fight a double war: one against the enemy, the other against starvation."*[xlvii] Such precaution was extremely sensible. In light of all of these considerations, Romanus' decision to send a robust force to Chliat appears an eminently sound tactic reflecting his deep military experience and judgement, so highly valued by his troops. However, the one crucial thing he misjudged was the capacity of the Doukai for treachery – as will soon become apparent.

Romanus then advanced on Manzikert itself. His advance was conducted with textbook precision. Before leaving Theodosiopolis, he ordered the army to find provisions for the next two months since it would be campaigning in *"uninhabited regions which had been utterly laid waste by the tribes (Turkmen)"*.[xlviii] When he reached Manzikert, the army built a fortified camp and palisade outside the city. Building well-defended camps was a central tenet of Byzantine military textbooks and a direct link to the discipline of the ancient Roman legions. He brought up siege engines *"transported on almost a thousand wagons"* and *"innumerable flocks and herds of animals"*[xlix] accompanied the army.

The Turks in Manzikert shot arrows from the ramparts at the advancing Byzantines while Romanus rode around the city walls, protected by a shield, looking for the best place to attack. Having found a suitable section of the walls, a regiment of Armenian infantry attacked it and, after battling all day, they broke through. The Turks hurriedly surrendered, sending envoys begging for their lives if they handed the city over. Romanus, *"elated by this turn of events"*[l] wanted to occupy the city that night but the Turks were worried that they would be killed in the confusion of the night and wanted to delay until the morning. Romanus rejected this and led more troops out to attack the city, whereupon the Turks agreed to surrender immediately.

Romanus treated the defeated Turks honourably, even allowing them to pass through the city gates fully armed. While Romanus maintained strict discipline in the Byzantine ranks, for example punishing a soldier caught stealing a Turkish donkey by cutting off his nose, he was still the army's favourite, and his capture of Manzikert quickly and with few casualties was celebrated by the soldiers outside the city, who greeted him with *"hymns of praise, acclamations and cries of triumph"*.[li]

Romanus had every reason to feel pleased. His capture of Manzikert had been brilliantly executed. Now, he could advance on Chliat, join Trachaneiotes and reunite the army, and face the Sultan in battle if Alp Arslan was feeling brave enough to face the largest Byzantine army that had been fielded that century. But just as he had every reason to feel confident, it was at this point that his carefully made plans began to unravel.

This began with news that Seljuk forces had attacked Byzantine foraging parties. Romanus sent out one of his senior generals, Nicephorus Bryennius, commander of the western army, with a large force to beat the Turks back. Bryennius encountered a more determined Turkish attack than he had expected, with groups of Turkish cavalry advancing across a wide front. There were confused melées, which the Turks seemed to be getting the better of, especially as they could use their archery skills against the Byzantine cavalry.

Bryennius sent messengers back to camp, asking for reinforcements. Romanus' initial reply was dismissive. He thought that the enemy facing Bryennius was only a handful of raiders since he still believed that Trachaneiotes' forces were blocking the Turkish advance from Chliat. However, he changed his mind as further reports of intense fighting came in. Acknowledging that the Turkish forces seemed surprisingly substantial, he sent Nikephorus Basilakes, the Dux of Theodosiopolis, to join Bryennius with a large group of Byzantine cavalry.

Basilakes was an Anatolian aristocrat, champing at the bit to meet the Turks in battle and take revenge on their brutal sacking of so many Byzantine cities. He immediately led his cavalry out into the open ground where the Turks were attacking Bryennius' men. The Turks retreated and Basilakes, jubilant with his apparent success, rode past Bryennius' soldiers, in pursuit of them. This proved to be a fatal mistake since the Turks, masters of the feigned retreat, pulled their horses round and surrounded the Byzantine cavalry. The result was carnage. The Byzantines were cut to pieces. Basilakes was himself unhorsed, surrounded and taken prisoner.

When news of this reached the Byzantine camp, Romanus ordered the army to assemble and led it out to face the Turks, who melted away at the sight of such a substantial force. But at nightfall, they returned and made another assault, this time on the Oghuz Turkish mercenaries, who were stationed outside the Byzantine camp. Because the Oghuz Turks looked very similar to the Seljuks,[35] the result was chaos. Attaleiates says it was a moonless night. In the pitch-black darkness, the Byzantines couldn't make out who was attacking whom.

The Oghuz wanted to be let into the safety of the Byzantine camp but the Byzantine soldiers wouldn't let them in because they thought they were Seljuk Turks. The result was horrifying. The Seljuks slaughtered their Oghuz cousins. *"Death would be, so everyone felt, preferable to what we then witnessed,"* Attaleiates says. After massacring the Oghuz, the Seljuks couldn't break into the camp but galloped around it *"...yelling and screaming, shooting arrows and other missiles, making tremendous, horrifying noises from all sides..."*[lii]

The army spent a sleepless night. The next day there was another Seljuk attack. This time their target was the far bank of the river next to the Byzantine camp. It was a clever tactical move by the Seljuks since the Byzantines needed water from the river. But this time the Byzantines were better prepared. Although they had lost their proficiency as mounted archers, they still had infantry archers who showered the Turks on the riverbank with arrows, inflicting heavy casualties and driving them away.

---

35   They were essentially the same as the Seljuk Turkmen except they had not converted to Islam. They joined the Byzantine army in the 1060s when their raids across the Danube were defeated.

But just as this small victory was achieved, there was another setback. A group of the surviving Oghuz Turks, together possibly with some of the Pecheneg cavalry, switched sides to join the Seljuks. Michael Attaleiates takes credit for persuading Romanus to demand an oath of loyalty from those who remained. As a result, the rest of the Oghuz and Pechenegs stayed with the Byzantines, loyally fighting with them in the battle that was shortly to follow.

Romanus now realised that he was facing a major Seljuk force, commanded by the Sultan. This was actually the opportunity he'd been looking for: a chance to win a decisive victory. And there's no doubt that he was confident he could beat the Seljuks, just as he'd defeated similar Steppe nomads in the Balkans. But there was one mystery that he couldn't explain. What had happened to the troops led by Trachaneiotes?

Romanus sent messengers to Trachaneiotes, ordering him to return immediately and reunite the army for a decisive strike against the Seljuks. For a whole day, he waited for news that Trachaneiotes was on his way back. But his messengers couldn't find Trachaneiotes. He, and an important part of the Byzantine army, had vanished into thin air.

What had in fact happened was that Trachaneiotes and his Varangians, together with the Frankish/Norman mercenaries, and the Pechenegs, had retreated back towards Melitene. The reason for this is one of the greatest mysteries of the Battle of Manzikert. But there is one very plausible explanation: treachery. Trachaneiotes had almost certainly been persuaded to betray Romanus by the Doukai.

One relevant reason to believe this is that Trachaneiotes was given the coveted governorship of Antioch by the Doukai after Romanus' death in 1072. This was clearly a reward for something, and his desertion from Romanus would certainly seem to be a fitting reason. Presumably, he also persuaded the Norman mercenary, Roussel de Bailleul, and the Pechenegs to betray Romanus, something that was no doubt quite easy to do with the promise of Doukas gold.

This view is not at odds with the sources. Attaleiates effectively calls him a traitor when he describes his desertion: *"The coward* [Trachaneiotes] *took no account of his lord or even his duty."*[liii] Even the account by Nicephorus Bryennius junior (the grandson of Nicephorus Bryennius who was one of Romanus' generals at Manzikert and whose account tries to portray the Doukai in a good light)[36] describes Trachaneiotes as *"completely discouraged"*[liv] which can be read as hostile to Romanus – so capable of treachery. In conclusion, there is sufficient evidence to suggest that Trachaneiotes was probably a traitor, or at best harboured some grudge against Romanus. However, his desertion wasn't sufficient by itself to result in defeat. Romanus still had a very substantial army with which to oppose the Sultan.

There was still one last chance to defeat the Turks.

---

36  There are three main Byzantine sources on the Battle of Manzikert, two favourable towards the Doukai and one against. This fraught historiography is discussed in Chapter 14.

# 11

# THE BATTLE OF MANZIKERT

Romanus wanted to strike against Alp Arslan as soon as possible. But he was still hoping that Trachaneiotes would return, completely unaware that he was already hundreds of miles away, fleeing in the opposite direction. Messengers sent to find him returned empty-handed. He then took the most momentous decision of his reign. He gave orders to prepare for battle the next day.

But just at that moment he received an unexpected message. At the gates of the Byzantine camp was a Seljuk delegation from Alp Arslan asking for an audience. The delegation was led by one of the Caliph of Baghdad's principal dignitaries, al-Muhalban, who was already well known to the Byzantines.

Romanus allowed the delegation to enter the camp, giving them an imperial cross as their passport for safe passage. When they proposed a truce, Romanus was initially elated.[lv] Not surprisingly there was a sense of triumph on the Byzantine side that the Seljuks were seeking peace. It provides a revealing insight into Alp Arslan's mind. While there was probably some gamesmanship on his part, since a truce would give him time to bring up more troops, it is also testimony to his respect for Romanus and his army.

Nevertheless, Romanus and his Anatolian supporters decided that it was a trick and that the Sultan was stalling for time.[lvi] In the end, he behaved haughtily, forcing the Arabs to prostrate themselves in his presence, a ritual called *proskynesis*.[37] He demanded that the Turks abandon their camp and retreat further away before he would even consider discussing a truce. Dismayed, the peace envoys departed.

On the next day, 26 August 1071, before the Seljuks could even respond to Romanus' request, he ordered the army to prepare for battle in the early morning. The Turks watched the Byzantine army assemble in the dusty plain outside Manzikert. They were impressed by the sight of the disciplined ranks of Cappadocian and Anatolian soldiers, so much so that Attaleiates says: *"...they [the Turks] were inclined to flight when they saw the Roman phalanxes all drawn up in ordered, disciplined battle array."*[lvii]

The Arab sources say the same. Although written decades after the event and with no eyewitness information, they claim that Alp Arslan was preparing to die in battle. He dressed in white so that his garb might serve as his shroud and he made his entourage swear to recognise his son, Malik-Shah, as his heir should he die in battle. Then, according to the Arab chroniclers, he made an impassioned speech to his army:

> *"No matter how few we may be, and no matter how great in numbers the Romans may be, I shall fling myself upon the enemy at this hour when the Moslems are praying for us... Either I shall be victorious and fulfil my goal or I*

---

37 This was an age-old ceremony, involving lying fully prostrate on the ground before the Emperor.

*shall be a martyr and enter Paradise. Those who desire*
*to follow me, come with me; those who wish to go back*
*may do so freely. There is here no Sultan commanding and*
*no soldier being commanded. For I am today only one of*
*you.*"[lviii]

While this passage was written a century after the battle, and
uses almost absurd poetic hyperbole, there's no doubt that
Alp Arslan's position was on the line. Now was his greatest
test. Defeat by the Byzantines would jeopardise his authority
over the Turkmen. The whole Seljuk Empire could very easily
unravel if Romanus won a victory. These thoughts must have
dominated his mind as he watched the Byzantines advance in
the morning sun.[38]

The bulk of the Seljuk army were the Turkmen. Although
historians commonly refer to 10,000 Kurdish cavalry joining
Alp Arslan before Manzikert, this is based on flimsy evidence.[39]
There may well have been some Kurdish troops, but the bulk
of the Seljuk army would have been the Turkmen living along
the Armenian border with Byzantium. They had been the
core of most Seljuk armies in the past and remained so at
Manzikert, as attested to by Attaleiates' numerous references
to the Turkish cavalry in the battle. There is no source that
provides any reliable indication of the size of the Seljuk army
but it seems reasonable to assume that it was a substantial
force, perhaps 30,000 strong.

Alp Arslan appointed one of his most trusted generals, a
eunuch called Taranges, to set about organising the Turkmen

---

38  Alp Arslan watched the whole battle from the safety of a hill overlooking the
    battlefield.
39  In fact, there is only one mention among Arab sources of the Kurdish cavalry
    who joined Alp Arslan, by Sibt Ibn al-Jawzi.

into a crescent formation facing the Byzantines so that they could harry them with arrows, and lure them into making charges similar to the disastrous foray that Nicephorus Basilakes had made two days earlier. However, he knew that victory could only be achieved if the Seljuks joined battle with the Byzantines, and this was far too risky unless an opportunity presented itself.

The Byzantines advanced in a battle order that certainly wasn't typical of the formations favoured by military manuals. These would have had infantry in the centre and cavalry on the wings. But such a conventional approach was totally impractical against the hit and run tactics of the Seljuks. Romanus knew this only too well since he was highly experienced at fighting steppe nomads and fully expected them to try to avoid a normal pitched battle. Therefore, he divided his army into four separate and self-sufficient battle groups, each containing a mix of infantry, heavy cavalry, archers and Pecheneg/Oghuz auxiliaries. As already discussed, no source mentions the Varangians and Normans being present at the battle, and it seems likely that they had been sent with Trachaneiotes to Chliat.

The advantage of Romanus' battle plan was the flexibility given to each battle group, allowing them to act independently of each other and to respond to the Turkish hit and run tactics in the most appropriate way. However, there was one major disadvantage. By giving such independence to the battle group commanders, Romanus lost much of his own control over the army. Successful coordination required good communication between the battle groups and a strong unity of purpose. The most effective way to achieve this would have been to have his most ardent supporters in charge of each of the battle groups. But this was where Romanus made an uncharacteristic mistake.

He put Andronicus Doukas in command of the rearguard with a mixed force of mercenaries and Byzantine troops. It remains a mystery why Romanus gave such a senior command to Andronicus, whose father he had exiled. Presumably he was trying to appease his critics by appearing lenient towards the Doukai. It is also possible that he had some personal respect for Andronicus who was by all accounts a dashing and brave young soldier. No doubt he also thought that the rearguard was the place where Andronicus could do least harm. He would soon learn that this was a mistake.

Romanus himself took personal command of the centre, which was almost certainly the power-house of the army, filled by the élite Cappadocian regiments, as alluded to by Attaleiates. On the right wing, he put one of his closest supporters, Theodore Alyates, another Cappadocian and fanatically loyal to Romanus. On the left wing was the western army led by its commander, Nicephorus Bryennius. Romanus was rightly confident that the western army would be loyal to him since he had been one of their most popular generals before he became Emperor, and they had sworn an oath of loyalty to him. However, their commander Bryennius, although not a traitor, was not one of his keenest supporters.

Although Byzantine casualties may have been quite high in Basilakes' disastrous cavalry charge two days before, Romanus' army was clearly still a large and powerful force, perhaps up to 30,000 strong in total. Choking in the dust kicked up by the huge numbers of horses' hooves,[40] emphasised by the Arab sources, the battle groups of the Byzantine army started to march across the plain towards the Seljuk camp, some five miles away. The two main Byzantine accounts of the battle

---

40   In the middle of summer, the ground would have been particularly dry and dusty.

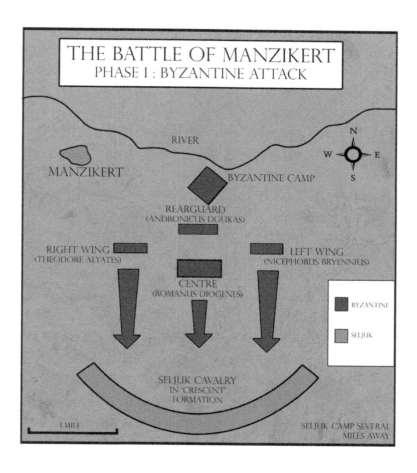

present different pictures. Attaleiates says the Turks melted away *"inclined to flight when they saw the Roman phalanxes all drawn up in ordered, disciplined battle array,"*[lix] while Bryennius junior says that the Seljuk general, Taranges, *"divided his army into several groups, set traps and organised ambushes, and ordered his men to surround the Byzantines and riddle them with arrows. The Byzantines, seeing their cavalry under attack, were obliged to follow it, which they did, while the enemy pretended to flee. But, falling victim to the traps and ambuscades, they suffered great losses."*[lx]

The truth probably lies somewhere between the two accounts. Attaleiates wasn't actually on the battlefield himself since he had remained behind in the Byzantine camp at Manzikert, as a non-combatant. Bryennius' grandfather was of course commanding the left wing of the army and would have known exactly what happened, and might well have left some records. Therefore, it's probably correct that Turkish resistance was stronger than Attaleiates makes out, with a good deal of skirmishing as the Byzantines advanced. It seems that Romanus' advance guard may have captured a Seljuk forward position,[41] but as he led the army across several miles of scrubland towards the main Seljuk camp, the Seljuks used typical Steppe nomad battle tactics and skilfully withdrew without committing to battle.

Attaleiates says that Romanus pursued the Turks until the evening when he became worried that they might circle round and try to attack the Byzantine camp which was poorly defended, *"stripped bare of soldiers, including foot sentries"*.[lxi] Therefore, he halted the centre and ordered the signal to be

---

41    There is mention in minor sources of the empty Seljuk camp itself being taken by Romanus but this almost certainly refers to a forward position rather than the main camp.

given to those on the wings to turn around and head back to camp. Romanus must certainly have felt frustrated that he hadn't brought Alp Arslan to a pitched battle but he had at least won a victory of sorts by forcing the Seljuks to retreat several miles.

It was then that things went disastrously wrong for Romanus. In the Byzantine army, the order to return to camp was given by reversing the imperial battle standards. The problem was that this signal could be open to misinterpretation. On this occasion, it seems that the soldiers on both wings weren't completely sure why the banners in the centre had been reversed. This facilitated the second act of treachery. Attaleiates has left us with a full description of what happened, which was so important that it is worth quoting in full:

> "...he [Romanus] *ordered the imperial banner to be turned around as a signal for the troops to return to camp. But when those soldiers who were far from the main body saw the imperial banner being turned around, they thought that the Emperor had fallen in defeat. Many relate that one of those who was waiting for a chance to get at him, a cousin of the Emperor's stepson Michael* [Andronicus Doukas] *who had previously plotted against him, spread this report among the soldiers. He* [Andronicus] *quickly got his men together – for the Emperor, with his good heart, had entrusted a large contingent to this man's command – and fled back to the camp. The nearest units followed his example and one by one they turned to flight without a fight, and others followed after them. When the Emperor saw this irrational flight and desertion, he took a stand with his own men, trying in the usual way to check the flight of his men, but nobody was listening to him."*[lxii]

Andronicus' treachery created a moment of confusion that was exactly what Alp Arslan had been hoping for. The Seljuks were the masters of opportunism in warfare. Their battle tactics could only be successful if they took advantage of disarray whenever it occurred. Their most important victory to date had been achieved in just this way at the Battle of Dandanqan in 1040, when the Ghaznavid army had been quarrelling over the use of a well. The situation at Manzikert now presented a very similar opportunity. Alp Arslan ordered an all-out attack. The mass of Seljuk cavalry facing the Byzantines stopped shooting arrows, drew their sabres and maces and charged. Romanus had got the pitched battle he wanted. But with the bulk of his army fleeing the field, the result was chaos.

The situation on the battlefield rapidly turned against the Byzantines. The right wing, led by Alyates, was subjected to a brutal Seljuk assault and started to break up. The centre, under Romanus' command, was holding firm but becoming isolated. Andronicus' rearguard was fleeing from the battlefield as fast as possible. The western army, on the left wing, and led by Bryennius, was holding its own against the Turkish onslaught as it retreated in good order. Bryennius junior emphasises that it tried to come to the Emperor's aid but was prevented from saving Romanus by ferocious Turkish resistance. However, his description, written fifty years after the battle, looks like an attempt to flatter his grandfather's memory since we know that the western army survived Manzikert largely intact, suggesting that it did not attempt too hard to save Romanus and instead chose to withdraw in reasonable order from the battlefield. We can assume that although Bryennius senior was not a downright traitor, his allegiance to Romanus was limited. When he saw that Romanus was surrounded, he

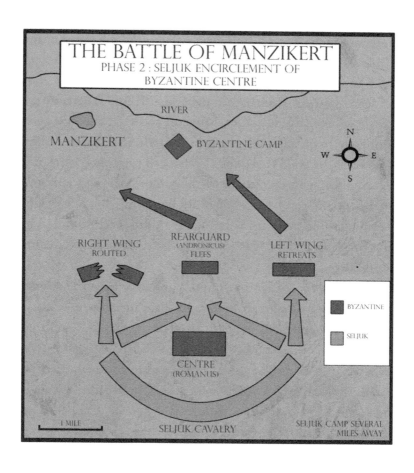

decided that it was best to save his troops while he could by retreating from the battlefield.

Romanus was now in a desperate position. With two of his four battle groups withdrawing from the battlefield, he and the centre were surrounded. Alyates' Anatolian soldiers on the right wing were the only ones that genuinely tried to rescue Romanus and, like him, they faced the full brunt of the Turkish attack and were pushed back as they tried to link up with the Emperor.

Surrounded, Romanus fought like a lion. There isn't a single source, Byzantine or Muslim, pro-Romanus or anti-Romanus, which doesn't praise him as a hero. Surrounded by the Turks, he tried to make his way back towards Manzikert. The fighting wore on into the evening. Alp Arslan concentrated more and more of his soldiers on stopping Romanus from escaping. Finally, with his horse shot dead, and wounded in the hand so that he was unable to hold a sword, Romanus surrendered.

Back in the Byzantine camp, panic reigned. The fleeing troops clustered outside the camp palisade. No one knew what had happened. Some said that Romanus had been killed while others said he had defeated the Turks. Groups of retreating soldiers suddenly appeared from the battlefield. Attaleiates says he tried to stop them and order them to fight but even groups of Romanus' favourite Cappadocian soldiers started to run away. Then he says that a large group of Byzantine cavalry suddenly appeared (maybe these were detachments of the western army that was withdrawing in reasonably good order), saying they didn't know whether the Emperor was dead or alive. After that the Turks arrived. Then it was everyone for himself as the troops abandoned the camp. Attaleiates sums it up vividly:

*After the fall of the Western Roman Empire, the Emperor Justinian I (527–565), depicted in this sixth-century mosaic in Ravenna, led an Eastern Roman revival, reconquering Italy and North Africa from the Goths and Vandals, as well as building some of the greatest late Roman monuments, including Hagia Sophia. (akg-images)*

The massive walls of Constantinople, first built by the Emperor Theodosius in the fifth century, changed the course of history by protecting both the Byzantine capital and the European hinterland from a series of invasions from the East. This photo shows a section of the partially restored walls. (Alamy)

Hagia Sophia in Constantinople was the centre of Byzantium and still dominates modern Istanbul. Built by the Emperor Justinian I between 532 and 537, its vast dome was the largest structure in Europe for nearly a thousand years. The four minarets are later Turkish additions. (akg-images)

*Basil II (976–1025), depicted wearing chain-mail armour, is often seen as one of the strongest Byzantine soldier-Emperors. In fact, he viewed much of the Byzantine army as a threat to his authority, and replaced many of its elite troops with mercenaries who he regarded as more loyal.*

*(akg-images)*

*Turkish horse archers, as shown in this Chinese painting of a steppe-nomad, represented a new and terrifying enemy for the Byzantines. According to a Byzantine source: "…the arrow in its course strikes either rider or horse, fired with such tremendous force that it passes clean through the body." (akg-images)*

*The Turks were nomadic warriors from the Asiatic steppe-land, as shown in this picture of the Russian steppes with the Altai mountains in the background. (Alamy)*

*The Emperor Romanus IV Diogenes revived the Byzantine army and led a powerful force into Armenia where he fought the Seljuk Sultan, Alp Arslan, at the Battle of Manzikert in 1071. He was winning the battle until a jealous rival betrayed him by withdrawing his forces, leaving Romanus surrounded by the Turks. In Margaret Dovaston's (1884–1954) painting, he is shown with an arrow in his upper arm, when contemporary sources say he was badly wounded in his right hand.*

*(Alamy)*

The four leaders of the First Crusade are shown in this woodcut after a drawing by Alphonse de Neuville (1835–1885): Godfrey of Bouillon, Raymond of Toulouse, Bohemond of Antioch and Tancred of Hauteville. (akg-images)

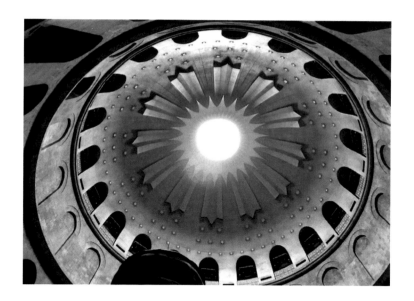

To pray beneath the dome of the Church of the Holy Sepulchre in Jerusalem (shown above) was every crusader's ultimate aim. The dome was originally built by the Romans, re-built by the Byzantines, and restored as recently as the 1990s. (Author's photo)

The crowning moment of the First Crusade was the capture of Jerusalem on 15 July 1099, after more than 400 years in Muslim hands, as depicted in Emile Signol's (1804–1892) painting. Many crusaders believed that their victory would trigger a divine apocalypse. Jerusalem was re-taken by Saladin in 1187. (Author's photo)

*Christ's stern face and threatening gaze in this late eleventh–century Byzantine mosaic (Dafni Monastery in Athens) is now regarded as one of the greatest artistic creations of the early Middle Ages. His severe expression may reflect the dire condition of the Byzantine Empire at the time. (Author's photo)*

*Another outstanding Byzantine mosaic is this depiction of Christ in Hagia Sophia in Istanbul. Made in the thirteenth century, the expression of intense humanity and emotional realism is regarded as an inspiration for the Italian Renaissance. (Author's photo)*

*"It was like an earthquake with howling, grief, sudden fear, clouds of dust and, finally, hordes of Turks riding all around us… The enemy chased us, killing some, capturing some and trampling others underfoot."*[lxiii]

The broken right wing of the army, commanded by Alyates, fled in disorder, pursued by the Turks. Even some of the Cappadocian soldiers in the centre appear to have abandoned the Emperor: *"Finally, many of the Kappadokians who were with the Emperor, one group after another, began to desert…"*[lxiv]

Meanwhile, the traitor Andronicus was speeding back to Constantinople as fast as his horse would carry him, not having drawn a sword. Trachaneiotes was also already hundreds of miles to the west, his forces of Varangians and Normans intact. The western army under Nicephorus Bryennius was also retreating, no doubt after suffering casualties, but still largely in one piece.

Back on the battlefield, Romanus and his remaining Cappadocians fought on. They must have made a miserable sight – with corpses littering the ground, men screaming in agony from their wounds, horses neighing in their death throes and blood soaking the ground. We will never know the real truth of what really happened. But by nightfall, the last survivors of the Byzantine centre surrendered.

Romanus' surrender is steeped in Islamic myth. Most medieval Muslim chroniclers delight in telling a tale that became legendary across Islam – that a lowly slave soldier, a Ghulam, took Romanus prisoner. Many versions of the story exist, and although the details vary, they all agree that as this simple soldier was about to kill Romanus, he suddenly realised who he was. Some say the Ghulam spoke Greek and Romanus told him: *"Hold your sword, for I am the Emperor of the Romans.*[lxv] Others say that the Ghulam saw his gilded armour and realised that he was a nobleman. Whatever the details given in the story, the message is always the same: Islam humbles the proud.

Aside from the symbolism that Alp Arslan's victory was to acquire in later years, there was one incontrovertible truth at the time: Romanus' plans to save Byzantium had been shattered. The new eastern army that he had painstakingly created over the last three years had been completely routed and largely destroyed. He himself was a prisoner of the Seljuk Sultan and the first Emperor to be taken prisoner for nearly three centuries.

# 12

# CIVIL WAR

Alp Arslan didn't realise he had captured the Emperor until the next day. When he was brought before him, he didn't believe it really was Romanus. He had his identity checked with the other Byzantine prisoners. Still distrustful, he asked the peace envoys that he had sent to Romanus only two days before, to confirm it really was him.

Once he was sure that the bloodied, wounded soldier kneeling before him was the Roman Emperor, he stood up from his throne and walked towards him. Romanus must have expected the worst. The last Byzantine Emperor to be captured had been beheaded and his skull made into a drinking cup.[42]

But Alp Arslan was no ordinary leader. He stopped in front of Romanus. He told his guards to raise him to his feet. Then to everyone's astonishment, he offered him his hand in friendship. Alp Arslan's chivalrous behaviour to Romanus counts as one of the most unexpected and extraordinary twists in the story of Manzikert. Like the legend of Romanus' capture by the slave soldier, it was to became legendary across Islam

---

42   This was the fate of Nicephorus I, defeated at the Battle of Pliska in AD 811, by the Bulgarian Khan, Krum.

as a symbol of Islamic moral superiority over Christianity. However, there is no doubt that it is true since every single account of Manzikert, both Byzantine and Arab, stresses his extraordinary magnanimity. Even Michael Psellus admits it grudgingly, his prose shivering with indignation as he recounts Romanus' unexpected escape from death. *"The commander-in-chief of the enemy forces* [Alp Arslan]... *celebrated his victory with a moderation that was beyond all expectation. Offering his condolences to the captive, he shared his own table with him,* [and] *treated him as an honoured guest..."*[lxvi]

Alp Arslan welcomed Romanus like a friend. He said the battle had been too close to call and that it could easily have gone the other way had he not been let down by his own side. In particular, he admired Romanus' bravery in battle and the honesty with which he spoke to his captor. When he asked Romanus what he would have done had he won the battle, and their positions had been reversed, Romanus is reputed to have said: *"...if I took you prisoner I would prepare a dog's collar for you."*[lxvii] To which the Sultan laughed: *"But I will not imitate your severity or harshness."*[lxviii]

Alp Arslan's generosity to Romanus achieved mythical status in the Islamic world over the next few centuries, but the truth is that Alp Arslan, astute as ever, had very good reasons to treat Romanus well. First, he wanted Byzantium as, in effect, a vassal state on his north-western border. Second, although he treated him with great honour and generosity, he demanded some major concessions.

To understand Alp Arslan's motives, we need to look more closely at what victory at Manzikert really meant for him. Most importantly, it gave him unparalleled authority over the Turkmen tribes. There were no further Turkmen insurrections during his reign. By contrast, defeat at Manzikert would certainly have caused a rapid loss of Turkmen support for the Seljuks, and the collapse of his empire.

The next most important consequence was the reassertion of his authority over the Baghdad Caliphate and the Sunni Arab world over which he ruled with fragile control. While this was not in doubt before Manzikert, defeat would have jeopardised his position in Baghdad just as much as it would have done with the Turkmen. So, Alp Arslan was now at the apex of his power. He also knew the battle had genuinely been a close call. He had every reason to thank Allah for victory.

It is equally important to understand that Manzikert didn't change Alp Arslan's longer-term strategy in the slightest. This remained the extension of Sunni Seljuk power southwards over the Shi'ite Fatimids in Syria, and ultimately Egypt. Within this context, having Byzantium as, in effect, a vassal state, and its Emperor as an obedient servant, would be helpful.

Although Romanus was treated like royalty, the peace settlement Alp Arslan forced upon him was far from generous. The Byzantine sources say little about the peace terms that were agreed but the Arab sources provide more detail, although sometimes conflicting. The essential elements were that Romanus had to surrender the key cities of Manzikert, Antioch, Edessa and Hierapolis, effectively stripping away the main line of defence of the Byzantine provinces in Anatolia. Next, he had to pay a huge ransom and ongoing tribute. According to one of the most reliable of the Muslim chroniclers,[lxix] this was originally set at ten million gold pieces, which Romanus negotiated down to one and a half million on the basis that the Byzantine treasury had been emptied to pay for the war. In addition, an annual tribute of 360,000 dinars was agreed. Finally, a marriage alliance was agreed for the future, preferably once Romanus had a daughter who could be married to Alp Arslan's oldest son (Romanus had two existing sons with the Empress Eudocia but he never had a daughter).

Nevertheless, however tough the terms, Alp Arslan was relaxed about enforcing them. It was more important to have Romanus as a vassal than impoverishing and humiliating him. Both men knew that Romanus' own future was uncertain. Therefore, Alp Arslan kept him in captivity for as short a time as possible. It was only eight days before he sent him back with the other Byzantine prisoners, including Nicephorus Basilakes, who had been captured before the main battle. Romanus and Alp Arslan parted as the best of friends. *"The only assurance the Emperor gave him* [i.e. to Alp Arslan] *was a strong handshake and then they parted, the Sultan releasing him to return to his own empire with many embraces and farewell honours."*[lxx]

Romanus' fears about his future proved well founded. On his way back to Manzikert, he found the town was still held by Byzantine soldiers. But they fled before he arrived, suggesting that they were allied with Andronicus. Honouring his treaty with Alp Arslan, Romanus handed Manzikert over to the Seljuks.

Then he rode on to Theodosiopolis, where only a month before he had held his council of war to decide the objectives of the campaign. He must have reflected on the extraordinary volatility in his fortunes. We know little about what physical condition Romanus was in. He had certainly been badly wounded in the hand at the Battle of Manzikert and this must still have been causing him pain. He rested there for several days, finding new clothes and armour to replace the Turkish ones he was wearing, while he pondered what to do next.

Deciding to return to Constantinople, he left Theodosiopolis dressed in imperial regalia and marched across northern Anatolia along the shortest route back to Constantinople. He gathered what survivors from Manzikert he could find *"…but he came across very few soldiers who were refugees from the battle."*[lxxi] This is testimony to the slaughter of most of the Cappadocian and Armenian soldiers at the Battle of Manzikert. And now he needed them more than ever. For when he arrived at a hill fort called Melissopetrion, near to Koloneia, he learned that a new Emperor had been proclaimed in Constantinople.

## The Doukai Seize Power

Back in the capital, no one actually knew what had happened to Romanus after the disaster at Manzikert. The most prevalent view was that he was dead. Or that if he had been captured, he was as good as dead. Even his great supporter, the senator Michael Attaleiates, had given up hope. He fled to Trebizond on the Black Sea coast where he, and a large part of the most senior non-combatants, including many senators, took a ship back to Constantinople.

It is at this point that Michael Psellus' account of events is more comprehensive than Attaleiates', since not only was he resident in Constantinople at the time but he also witnessed the palace coup that happened. He says that within a few days of the battle, news of the defeat was brought by the first survivors. Then more arrived. But they all had different versions of the battle. Some thought Romanus was dead; others that he'd been taken prisoner.

The Senate wondered what to do in this situation? It was assumed that Romanus would not return. Power was still in the hands of the Empress Eudocia but Psellus describes the growing tension between her and the senators as to whether she should rule alone or jointly with her son, Michael. Psellus is at pains to paint a picture of Michael as being the epitome of modesty and respect for his mother. But the truth is that Psellus' description is carefully contrived propaganda (discussed more fully in Chapter 14) to conceal the brutal palace coup that the Doukai were planning. To achieve this, Caesar John, previously exiled to his estates in Bithynia by Romanus, rushed back to Constantinople.

The crucial moment came when news that Romanus was still alive reached the capital. According to Psellus, Eudocia received a letter from Romanus himself *"telling her of his adventures"*.[lxxii] What could Eudocia do? The sources are confusing on this point. Both Psellus and Attaleiates record that she was initially reluctant to support Romanus. This is particularly surprising coming from Attaleiates given that he said she still loved him when he left Constantinople for the Manzikert campaign. So, how should we read this?

The most plausible interpretation seems to be that she was concealing her support for Romanus since she knew that Caesar John was poised to seize power. By showing reservations about Romanus, she hoped to appease Caesar John while she worked out a way to restore him to the imperial throne. But the Doukai acted too fast and ruthlessly for her. It was exactly this kind of cut-throat Machiavellian politics that Caesar John excelled at. He immediately despatched his two sons, Andronicus and Constantine, to bribe the Varangian guard, the main body of troops remaining in the city, to proclaim Michael Emperor.

Suitably paid off, the Varangians did just that: *"...the guards* [the Varangians] *banged on their shields all together, bawled their heads off as they shouted their war cry, clashed sword on sword..."*[lxxiii]

Seeing the bearded Vikings taking over the palace, Eudocia thought she would be killed: "[Eudocia] *did indeed lose her nerve, and pulling her veil over her head she ran off to a secret crypt below ground."* The Varangians pursued her and dragged her away to be exiled to a convent. Psellus says that the new Emperor Michael VII refused to ratify his mother's cruel treatment, and maybe that was true, but it made no difference since Caesar John and his two sons were now back in control. The traitors of Manzikert had won.

## CIVIL WAR

Romanus learned of this palace coup when he reached the central Anatolian city of Amasea. He immediately occupied a nearby fortress, Dokeia, and made this his headquarters as he pondered what to do next. The army he had with him was a small force, certainly incapable of taking Constantinople. He was almost certainly still suffering from his wounds at Manzikert.

While Romanus prevaricated, Caesar John despatched his son, Constantine, against him with what soldiers he could put together. These were principally the troops who had deserted from Manzikert under Andronicus and Trachaneiotes. But importantly, they didn't include the western army, commanded by Bryennius at Manzikert, since it refused to join the Doukai against Romanus who had been their former commander: "*The soldiers of the West, for their part, had denounced the breaking of faith with him* [Romanus], *for they had been secured with oaths in advance never to consent to any acts done against him."*[lxxiv]

As such, the Doukas army must have been quite small, consisting of Varangians, Pechenegs and levies from the

Doukai estates. Romanus' forces were a match for these, at least initially, especially since the majority of the Franks and Normans went over to his side.[lxxv] In a number of skirmishes, Romanus' troops got the better of the Doukai, but then two things happened which changed everything. The first was the appearance in Constantine Doukas' army of a Norman knight called Crispin who nursed a particular grudge against Romanus. This was because he was the same man who had rebelled against Romanus in 1069, and who Romanus had subsequently imprisoned at Abydos (see Chapter 7). Caesar John, the master of opportunism, released him and persuaded him to join the Doukai with the job of winning over Romanus' Norman mercenaries.

Then, Romanus was unlucky with timing. Just as Crispin arrived, he left for Cappadocia to recruit more soldiers. Leaving one of his most trusted commanders, Theodore Alyates, in command of the army, he had no reason to suppose that this would create a problem. Alyates was one of his most loyal supporters, having commanded the right wing at Manzikert and a Cappadocian himself. He was an impressive soldier, according to Attaleiates: "...*a man from a family distinguished in warfare and who was impressive to behold, as he was exceptional in size and height and had shown his mettle in many campaigns.*"[lxxvi]

But Crispin was to prove more than his match. The Doukas army advanced towards Alyates' camp at Dokeia, prompting him to launch an attack. In the battle that followed, Alyates underestimated Crispin's influence over his own Norman mercenaries who deserted to join Crispin because he was "*...speaking to the Franks in their own language.*"[lxxvii] The result was a rout. The Norman cavalry charge shattered the Cappadocian battle line. The Cappadocians fled the field. Alyates himself was captured. His eyes were then gouged out with tent pegs in the brutal blinding so beloved of the Byzantines.

This defeat had a profound effect on Romanus. Alyates was a close friend and his blinding seems to have particularly disheartened Romanus: *"When he learned of this* [his brutal blinding] *Diogenes felt a deep sorrow."*[lxxviii] He retreated with the remaining Cappadocian soldiers to a hilltop fort in Cappadocia called Tyropoios. For the first time in his long and difficult reign, Romanus appears to have lost heart. It must be remembered that he was still suffering from his wounds sustained at Manzikert and was almost certainly incapable of holding a sword let alone fighting in battle. Up until the Battle of Manzikert, Romanus had always led from the front and enjoyed being in the thick of battle. After Manzikert, he was a shadow of his former self.

Attaleiates claims that he missed a huge opportunity to strike back at the Doukai when Constantine Doukas' army retired back to Constantinople, leaving Anatolia open to Romanus to reclaim. But instead of doing this, he retreated east towards Antioch to join forces with the governor of Antioch. This man was an Armenian noble called Chatatourios, who Romanus had previously appointed to the position. A staunch supporter of Romanus, he had refused to comply with the Doukai instructions to march against him and instead put at his disposal what was in effect the last remnants of the regular Byzantine army in the east – the garrison of Antioch and the Byzantine forces along the Syrian border. These soldiers were probably mainly Armenians, some of whom might have fought at Manzikert. Romanus was also hoping for Turkish support since Alp Arslan had promised to send him Turkish troops from neighbouring Syria.

## The Defeat and Death of Romanus

But Romanus was a broken man. He made a series of tactical mistakes, starting with his failure to intercept the army the Doukai sent against him in the spring of 1072, as it made its way through the winding passes and clifftops of the Cilician mountain in south-eastern Turkey. Commanded by Andronicus, the traitor of Manzikert, Attaleiates says that Romanus could easily have prevented this army crossing the Taurus Mountains since he held the mountain passes.

In May 1072, this army passed safely through the Taurus Mountains and marched out into the plain beside the fort of Adana where Romanus and Chatatourios were camped. Romanus didn't take part in the ensuing battle in which Chatatourios was captured. Yet again it was Crispin and the Normans who played the key role. They charged the Byzantine forces and smashed their battle line, forcing them into a headlong retreat.

In the rout, Chatatourios was captured and humiliated by Andronicus' soldiers who stripped him of his clothes and brought him before Andronicus *"naked and wretched both on account of his present condition and the harm that he was about to suffer"*.[lxxix] Psellus claims that Andronicus was magnanimous to his captive but we can assume that this was fiction since Chatatourios disappears from history.

Romanus remained in the fort of Adana with what remained of his troops. Psellus says he was hoping for troops to arrive from the Sultan and was ultimately betrayed by his own men. Attaleiates describes a more likely scene: *"…the two sides negotiated with each other and they agreed that Diogenes would divest himself of his imperial claim along with his hair, and thus he would live out the rest of his life as a monk."*[lxxx]

Attaleiates emphasises the sadness of Romanus' supporters as they saw him surrender to the treacherous Andronicus: *"At that moment many who witnessed this sight* [Romanus' surrender] *felt a horrible and irresistible fear combined with pity... For they were all men who had often campaigned with him, made up the company of his bodyguards, had celebrated his reign as blessed..."*[lxxxi]

The hideous crime that happened next was to haunt Byzantium for centuries afterwards. The truth is that Romanus would have been better advised to commit suicide, as his father had done when arrested for treason, rather than face the retribution that Andronicus was planning for him. Returning to Constantinople, Andronicus put him on a donkey, with his hair cut and dressed in black as a monk. He paraded him through the Anatolian villages and towns in this wretched state. Attaleiates says that he also poisoned him so that he became ill, with severe stomach cramps.

Worse was to come. Although Romanus had surrendered on condition that he became a monk and was guaranteed his safety, Caesar John wasn't prepared to take any chances. He decided that he should be blinded, the normal punishment which the Byzantines inflicted on traitors and political rivals.

When Romanus heard this, he panicked. He made one last desperate plea to the bishops who had brokered his surrender to Andronicus. There were three of them – the Bishops of Chalkedon, Herakleia and Koloneia. Attaleiates says they tried to stop Andronicus' men from seizing Romanus but it was to no avail. He was led away, protesting and calling out for the bishops to save him. Andronicus' men then pinned him down while one of them drove a poker into his eyes as he screamed. Attaleiates describes the horrific scene:

*"They put him in a small room and… tied down his four limbs and many men held him down with shields on his chest and stomach. Then they… used an iron pin to destroy his eyes in an extremely painful and cruel way while he roared and bellowed like a bull, though no one took pity on him… When he arose his eyes were drenched with blood, a pitiable and pathetic sight that made everyone who saw it cry uncontrollably."*[lxxxii]

With his horrific injuries, he was mocked and carried backwards on a donkey to the Bosphorus to take a boat to a monastery he himself had founded on the island of Prote. Whether he got there or not is uncertain. Psellus says that he died shortly after arriving at the monastery but Attaleiates suggests he died on the way there, saying that his brutal blinding left him *"…like a rotting corpse with his eyes gouged out, his head all swollen up and maggots visibly dropping off. A few days later he died in excruciating pain."*[lxxxiii]

Attaleiates was so shocked that he called for divine revenge on the Doukai.

*"As for you, O Emperor (Michael VII), what was this order that you gave…? One way or another, a day will come when an Evil Eye, Titanic and Kronian, will turn its gaze upon you and push your fortunes to the same evil fate."*[lxxxiv]

Attaleiates' words would prove to be true – not just for the Doukai but for the whole of Byzantium.

# 13

# THE COLLAPSE OF BYZANTIUM

After Romanus' death, Byzantium's collapse was rapid. The five years of rule by Michael VII must count as the most disastrous in the whole history of Byzantium. Complacency, arrogance and incompetence rapidly reduced the empire to a state of chaos from which it never truly recovered.

## THE REIGN OF MICHAEL VII DOUKAS

On 4 August 1072, Romanus died from his brutal blinding. In Constantinople, Caesar John celebrated. His nephew, Michael VII, was Emperor. Everything seemed to have gone his way. But the truth was that Byzantium could not have found an Emperor less suitable to face the enveloping crisis of the 1070s. In most ways, he was the exact opposite of Romanus. Still in his early twenties, with no military experience, he'd lived a secluded life in the palace. Tutored by sycophants like Michael Psellus, who taught him how to write iambic verses but little else, the later Byzantine chronicler, Skylitzes, described him thus: "*While he* [Michael VII] *spent his time in the useless pursuit of iambic and anapaestic verse, and they were poor efforts indeed, he brought his empire to ruin...*"[lxxxv]

Some historians even think he may have been mentally retarded. He was certainly incapable of ruling and passed all matters of government to a eunuch courtier, called Nikephoritzes, who so effectively put him under his spell that even Caesar John decided to withdraw to his estates in Bithynia. Meanwhile, the empire's enemies gathered on all sides. In the west, a serious revolt against imperial rule by the Bulgarians in 1072 was only just crushed by the western army, which had survived the Battle of Manzikert. Raids by the Pechenegs, and border disputes with the rapidly growing Kingdom of Hungary, also started to intensify. But the main threat in the west lay across the Adriatic since southern Italy had been lost to the Normans in 1071, when the last Byzantine stronghold of Bari fell. Now, Robert Guiscard, one of the most formidable soldiers in Europe, was pondering when best to strike at Byzantium. He was only kept at bay for the time being by the crafty diplomacy of the eunuch, Nikephoritzes, who devised a marriage betrothal between Guiscard's daughter and Michael VII's young son, Constantine.

But if the situation in the west was bad, in the east it was infinitely worse. There was no central military organisation left after Romanus' death. Garrisons still existed scattered among the cities and towns like Antioch and Edessa. But the Cappadocian heartland was wide open to Turkish attack. At first this was not disastrous since Turkmen plundering raids had abated in the months after Manzikert, as Alp Arslan had left strict instructions to honour the peace with Romanus.

However, when he heard of Romanus' brutal blinding he was enraged and ordered the Turkmen to resume raiding:

"*Alp Arslan, upon hearing of Romanus' blinding, directed his troops to take the land of the Greeks, and to shed the blood of the Christians.*"[lxxxvi] The Turkmen were only too pleased to comply and poured through what was left of the Byzantine defences.

The situation didn't change with Alp Arslan's untimely death. Campaigning in the east of his vast empire, he was killed by a rebellious provincial governor in Turkestan. The man was taken before the Sultan but had managed to conceal a dagger and rushed forward to stab him. The Arab chroniclers say that Alp Arslan, who took great pride in his reputation as an archer, motioned to his guards not to interfere. He drew his bow, but his foot slipped and the arrow missed, allowing the man to reach him and stab him in the chest. Alp Arslan died from this wound four days later in October 1072.

The deaths of both Romanus and Alp Arslan within three months of each other, and barely more than a year after the Battle of Manzikert meant the complete breakdown of any pretence of peace between the Byzantines and the Seljuks. However, even though the Turkmen drove their flocks into the heartlands of Byzantine Anatolia, there was no invasion initiated by Alp Arslan's successor, his son Malik-Shah. Indeed, just the opposite. Malik-Shah paid little attention to Byzantine Anatolia, focusing instead on fighting the Seljuks' two main enemies: the Qarakhanids to the east and the Fatimids to the west. This brought the Byzantines something of a breathing space as the Seljuk Turkmen fought in Syria and the Levant against the Fatimids.

Two Seljuk warlords, Artuq and Atsiz made good progress. They captured the Fatimid strongholds in Syria, one by one: first Aleppo, then Jerusalem (the brutal sacking of which attracted attention in Europe with Pope Gregory II promising to take up arms against the Turks in 1074) and finally, Damascus in 1075, before advancing into Egypt where Atsiz was crushingly defeated by the Fatimids in 1077 outside Cairo. The Seljuks never advanced into Egypt again.

## THE DOUKAI CAMPAIGN TO RECOVER ANATOLIA

With the Seljuks fighting the Fatimids, many of the main towns and cities of Byzantine Anatolia were able to hold out against the Turkmen, although the countryside was overrun by them forcing growing numbers of rural refugees to flee to Constantinople. This brought hunger, overcrowding and disease to the capital which even the incompetent government of Michael VII could not ignore. Belatedly, Michael VII's chief minister, Nikephoritzes yielded to public pressure to muster an army to confront the Turks. The problem was that with the corpses of Romanus' regiments still lying on the plains of Manzikert, there was no effective army to face them.

In 1073, Nikephoritzes appointed Isaac Comnenus to lead an army to Iconium in Cappadocia to confront the Turkmen. It consisted of low quality feudal levies of the Byzantine magnates, called the *Hetaireai*, and a mixture of mercenaries including the Varangians and several hundred Norman knights led by Roussel de Bailleul. Little did the Byzantines realise it but this Norman, Roussel, was about to become as dangerous to them as the Turks were. He was the Norman commander who had deserted Romanus at the Battle of Manzikert, and rose to prominence again when his fellow Norman, Robert Crispin (who had engineered Romanus' defeat), was poisoned by jealous rivals in 1072. He would soon show that his treacherous behaviour at Manzikert was capable of being repeated.

After advancing to Iconium, Roussel deserted Isaac and took his Normans to set up what was in effect his own principality in the old Armeniac theme (the north-eastern rim of Anatolia), with his base at Amasea. Roussel had almost certainly been planning this. He was copying the tactics of the Normans in southern Italy, who had turned from mercenaries to lords of their own fiefdoms.

Unwisely, Isaac ignored Roussel's desertion and marched to Caesarea, where he encountered a Turkish war band. His Byzantine soldiers were easily routed by the Turks and Isaac was taken prisoner. While the Doukai ransomed Isaac from Turkish captivity, Roussel took delight in extending his own fiefdom in Anatolia. Ironically, the Doukai felt more threatened by this Norman insurrection than by the Turkish invasion. It reminded them of what the Normans had done in southern Italy with devastating consequences for Byzantine authority. And this time it was even closer to home.

In 1074, another Byzantine army marched east. Led by no less than Caesar John himself, with his son, Andronicus, the traitor of Manzikert, the army advanced into central Anatolia. It was to be the last Byzantine army to venture this far east in the eleventh century. It marched past Amorium to cross the Sangarius River at the great bridge of Zompos, just as Romanus had done on his way to Manzikert in 1071. But this army was a shadow of the great host that Romanus had led to Manzikert. And Roussel was only too keen to meet it in battle. He and his band of Norman knights were waiting for the Byzantines on the other side of the bridge.

## THE BATTLE OF ZOMPOS BRIDGE

The Battle of Zompos Bridge drove the final nail into the coffin of Byzantine rule in Anatolia. With fifty per cent of the Byzantine army consisting of mercenaries, it was critically flawed, as became immediately apparent when the entire right wing of Frankish cavalry defected to Roussel in the first stage of the battle. Roussel encircled Caesar John and his Varangians in the centre. In a bizarre repeat of the pattern of events at Manzikert, it was the rearguard, commanded by Nicephorus Botaneiates, that ensured a complete Byzantine rout by retreating and abandoning the field. Botaneiates had little love for the Doukai, and his sense of self-preservation came into play when he saw that Caesar John's defeat was inevitable.

As a result, the traitors of Manzikert suffered the same fate that they had themselves inflicted on Romanus at Manzikert. Caesar John was surrounded by Roussel's Franks. Andronicus led the left wing of regular Byzantine troops in a desperate charge to save his father. But Roussel's Franks were more than a match for the Byzantines. Andronicus was unhorsed and badly wounded. Caesar John led a sally out to save his son, as the Franks were trying to take his helmet off to cut off his head. Andronicus just escaped death but they were both taken prisoner.

Crippled by his wounds, Andronicus would die three years later. Indeed, his wounds were so bad that he was immediately released by Roussel who kept Caesar John prisoner. Now, Roussel realised that he was in a strong enough position to seize the empire for himself. All the Franks in Byzantine pay flocked to join him. Leading a substantial force of some 3,000 Norman and Frankish knights, with no doubt several thousand infantry and non-combatants in support, Roussel advanced on Constantinople and set up camp at Chrysopolis, just across the Bosphorus from the capital.

## ROUSSEL'S BID FOR POWER

He then played his trump card. He demanded that Michael VII abdicate in favour of Caesar John who was to be his puppet Emperor. The farce of Doukas rule had come full circle to its humiliating conclusion. The empire was now being bartered for by a Norman mercenary. But Michael VII's government, run by the eunuch Nikephoritzes, still had one more card up their sleeves. Messengers were despatched to the most powerful of the Turkmen chieftains, Artuq, begging him to attack Roussel, with the promise of gold. As a result, a Turkmen army rode west to attack the Normans. One band of mercenaries had been recruited to fight another.

Roussel was not intimidated by the idea of a fight with the Turkmen. Indeed, he seemed to relish it. He immediately led his forces from Chrysopolis to meet the Turks in battle. At a place called Metabole, he met the Turkish advance guard. The Norman cavalry charge was the eleventh century equivalent of the twentieth-century German blitzkrieg, and the numerically smaller Norman force of some 3,000 knights sent the much larger Turkish force (Attaleiates says 6,000) reeling. But Roussel had underestimated the size of Artuk's war band. As the Normans continued to charge forward, they found themselves facing the main body of Turks. According to Attaleiates, this consisted of 100,000 Turkish cavalry (certainly an exaggeration although Attaleiates is not normally given to this).

He describes the heroic bravery of the Normans in the face of insurmountable odds: *"...Roussel spurred his Franks into an unbridled charge... whereupon he saw the mass of Turks, boundless in their multitude and heaving like the waves of a vast sea..."lxxxvii*

After fierce fighting, the Normans were defeated. Both Roussel and Caesar John were captured. Michael VII offered Artuq gold to ransom both of them. Caesar John was handed over to him. This time even the most Machiavellian of Byzantium's politicians couldn't escape disgrace. He agreed to step down from politics and become a monk. His head was shaved but, unlike Romanus, he escaped blinding. And indeed he would later return to politics for one last roll of the dice.

As for Roussel, he survived thanks to the efforts of his wife who acted quickly and decisively to save him.[43] She took command of the survivors of the Norman army who fled to the fortress of Metabole. There, she organised a successful defence, and managed to persuade the Turks to return her husband for a considerable amount of captured Byzantine gold.

## THE LOSS OF ANATOLIA

Roussel's revolt marks the beginning of a new era in Byzantine military history. Thereafter, there was no longer any pretence that a regular Byzantine army existed, capable of defending Anatolia. The use of Turk against Norman was an admission of complete military failure. The imperial army had ceased to exist except for the western army that had survived Manzikert

---

43   According to the Byzantines, Norman wives were as feisty as their husbands.

and a few garrisons still left in Antioch, Edessa and Trebizond on the Black Sea coast of Anatolia.[44]

Cappadocia and the rest of modern-day Turkey was now firmly in Turkish hands. Without an army to oppose them, the Turkmen spread across the length and breadth of Anatolia. They took control of most of the countryside of modern-day Turkey in the period up to 1078. But they couldn't take all of the towns and cities, or at least not immediately. Many of these continued to hold out so that a bizarre situation developed, with Turks appearing on the eastern banks of the Bosphorus, just a few miles from Constantinople, while 1,000 miles to the east, Antioch and Edessa in northern Syria continued to hold out.

## THE DOUKAI ARE OVERTHROWN

The next phase of Byzantine collapse resulted from a series of rebellions against the incompetent government of Michael VII. These began in 1077 with rebellions in both east and west. In the west, the western army under Nicephorus Bryennius revolted in a bid to seize the throne. Simultaneously, in the east, the most powerful of the surviving Asian magnates, Nicephorus Botaneiates, also rebelled. The race was on to see who could oust Michael VII the first.

The Byzantines not only destroyed their scarce resources fighting each other, but what was worse was their mortgaging of Anatolia to the Turks in return for their support. Botaneiates gave Sulayman control of a host of Anatolian towns in return for Turkish mercenaries – Pylae, Praenetus, Nicomedia,

---

44  A Byzantine nobleman, Theodore Gabras, led a revolt against the Turks who had captured the city in 1074, defeating them and recapturing the city.

Ruphinianae, Cyzicus, Chalcedon and Chrysopolis all appear to have passed into Turkish hands. Using Turkish forces, he ousted Michael VII, who agreed to abdicate and entered a monastery in March 1078.

## THE RISE OF ALEXIUS COMNENUS

The spate of rebellions between 1077 and 1081 is dizzying. Botaneiates' rule only lasted three years until he was himself confronted by new rebellions. The first was by the western army, still led by Nicephorus Bryennius, who had commanded it at Manzikert. This rebellion was defeated at the Battle of Kalavryai when a capable young general called Alexius Comnenus, commanding mainly Turkish mercenary troops, defeated the superior regular Byzantine forces of the western army through a mixture of luck and cunning. The tragedy was that the Byzantines succeeded in destroying the last remnant of their regular army. The line of descent from the legions of ancient Rome had finally come to an end.

The focus of attention now turned to this young general, Alexius Comnenus. A clever tactician and a brave soldier, he defeated another rebellion, this time by Nicephorus Basilakes, Romanus' erstwhile general who had been captured at Manzikert. But in 1081, the servant turned on his master. The young Alexius Comnenus marched on Constantinople.

It was then that Caesar John played his last hand. Seizing the opportunity to get his own back on Botaneiotes who had deposed Michael VII, Caesar John bribed the German mercenaries guarding a section of the walls of Constantinople to let Alexius's motley army of western mercenaries into the great city, which they proceeded to loot until Alexius was able to restore order. This was payment for Alexius' marriage to Eirene Doukas in 1078, the daughter of Andronicus Doukas. With Caesar John's sons, Andronicus and Constantine, both dead, this union offered the last hope of continuing the house of Doukas, united with that of the Comneni.

On 4 April, 1081, Alexius Comnenus was crowned Emperor. At long last, Byzantium had an Emperor who merited his position. He was a brave young general, resourceful, battle-hardened and determined. But he was the heir to a dying empire.

# 14

# REFLECTIONS ON THE REIGN OF ROMANUS DIOGENES

Before continuing with the subject of how Byzantium's decline came to ignite one of the most important events in medieval history – the Crusades – this chapter turns to a discussion of how Romanus Diogenes' reign has been misunderstood and his attempt to save Byzantium underestimated. For, as will become apparent, history has not been kind to the memory of Romanus Diogenes.

## UNCOVERING THE TRUTH ABOUT ROMANUS

Contemporary accounts are seldom objective. As Winston Churchill allegedly said: *"History is written by the victors."* In the context of eleventh-century Byzantium, his words have particular relevance since one of the most influential sources was in effect written by the victors over Romanus, that is the Doukas family – the traitors of Manzikert. Their version of events has distorted the truth about Romanus and it is time that the full extent of their deception was laid bare.

The source in question is *The Chronographia* written by Michael Psellus, who became the Doukas family's closest adviser after they overthrew Romanus, and the 'éminence grise' behind the disastrous reign of Michael VII Doukas. Written in the mid-1070s, it is a history of the Byzantine Emperors in the eleventh century. First published in English in 1953, there are a host of reasons for its popularity. It is very well written – lively and full of anecdotes. The characters – the majority of whom are the Emperors during the eleventh century – are vividly and amusingly portrayed. The writing is sharp and crisp. Michael Psellus himself was a charismatic figure – a highly successful lawyer and judge, he became a senator and was influential in political circles, and has long been highly regarded by historians for his diverse collection of works on philosophy, science and poetry. Scholars see him as one of the great medieval intellectuals, paving the way for the cultural creativity of the Italian Renaissance. So, it would seem only natural to assume that his description of Romanus' reign is likely to be accurate and insightful.

How wrong this is.

What does Psellus say about Romanus? In brief, he describes him as an arrogant fool who led the Byzantine armies to defeat due to his own incompetence. Indeed, his dislike of Romanus is so intense that he even opens his account of his reign with the startling statement that the Empress *"...should have put him* [Romanus] *to death"*.

However, it is now clear that Psellus' view is a gross and calculated misrepresentation. Not only is it contradicted point by point in the only other contemporary account of the period – *The History* – written by Michael Attaleiates, but new evidence has recently come to light showing Psellus to be a hypocrite of the most extraordinary proportions.

This new evidence consists of three panegyrics that he wrote during the reign of Romanus Diogenes.[lxxxviii] They provide an extraordinary revelation. The first was penned in early January 1068, a few days after Romanus' coronation, and presumably delivered in the Senate. Its praise for Romanus shows that Psellus was in fact one of his supporters when he became Emperor: *"Today is a day of salvation, today brings freedom from hardship… Today the Lord visited his domain and leaned over from the sky and saw, and dispatched his angel from on high and relieved us of present evil and future misfortune, of gathering clouds and arrow shots."*[lxxxix]

And this particular oration was no mistake, or anomaly, since we have two more in similar vein. The second tells of his admiration for Romanus' self-sacrifice in fighting the Turks:

> *"Your soul was not conquered by the decorations and the other trappings of ruling, or by the beauty of the crown. But in the same way you were crowned by God so that we live in luxury and happiness, you take care of us, toiling in all sorts of cares and pain, in the same way you were adorned with the crown, and you sharpened the edge of the sword against enemies."*[xc]

The third describes Psellus' hope that Romanus' campaigns would bring victory over the Turks.

> *"May a cloud covering your head protect you from the heat, may a pillar of light marching ahead of your shield guide you. May the Lord flatten for you every craggy and high mountain, fill for your sake the deep ravines and straighten*

*the narrow winding paths. Adorn your head with victory wreaths and return to us crowned with a thousand victories and glorified by numerous trophies.*"[xci]

Why then did Psellus change his mind so dramatically and malign someone whom he had previously so ardently supported?

The answer is that Psellus was a political chameleon. As a supporter of Romanus when he was in power, Romanus' defeat at Manzikert put him in a difficult position. The viciousness of his attack on Romanus in *The Chronographia* was an attempt to win favour with the Doukai – the new rulers – and erase memories of his previous support for Romanus. With the Doukai in power, there is no doubt that Psellus pandered to his new masters in the most glaringly deceitful way. While the reign of the Doukai from 1072 to 1078 is universally regarded as a time of unmitigated disaster for Byzantium, Psellus' description of these years is sycophantic, in particular depicting the grossly incompetent Emperor Michael VII Doukas as gifted and capable.

Unfortunately, we know nothing about Psellus' death but he probably died at some point between 1078 and 1081 since he disappears from history from 1078 onwards. When the Doukai were overthrown in 1078, there was an opportunity for an 'alternative' view about Romanus and Manzikert to be put forward. This took the form of Attaleiates' *The History*, which is an almost blow-by-blow rebuttal of everything that Psellus wrote.

Like Psellus, Attaleiates was a high-ranking lawyer and senator, and there are compelling reasons to believe that his account is more reliable than that of Psellus. He was actually present on all of Romanus' campaigns, including the last one that ended with the Battle of Manzikert. In contrast, Psellus was present only on the first campaign in 1068. Attaleiates' *The History* is a detailed account of Romanus' reign compared with Psellus' very cursory overview. Indeed, without it we would have almost no idea of the details of the Battle of Manzikert or Romanus' other campaigns. And since it would be difficult to make this level of detail up, we can assume that it is largely authentic.

Attaleiates' *The History* is also more analytical about the causes of Byzantine decline. While Psellus doesn't even acknowledge that the empire had shrunk within his own lifetime to a shadow of its former size, Attaleiates' work not only recognises this but also tries to rationalise why it happened. One of his most intriguing explanations lies with his comparison of modern Byzantines with their Republican Roman predecessors. He sees modern Byzantines as cowardly and foolish, suitable for God to punish. In contrast, the Republican Romans, although they had no knowledge of God, were, he argues, more genuinely pious in their pagan notions of honour, fortitude and courage, and therefore more deserving of God's patronage.

But the most striking feature of Attaleiates' work lies in his portrayal of Romanus as the exact opposite of that presented by Psellus. In the first of his campaigns, he praises how he made the Byzantines "...*stand up to their enemies...* [and] *recover their noble outlook...*"[xcii] His writing seethes with hatred for the Doukai's betrayal of Romanus and their part in his hideous death: "*As for you, O Emperor* [Michael VII]... *One way or another, a day will come when an Evil Eye, Titanic and Kronian, will turn its gaze upon you...*"

So, given the weight of evidence supporting Attaleiates' views, why is Psellus' account of Manzikert regarded as remotely credible even today? The answer lies partly with Byzantine politics, and in particular the role of the Comneni, who ruled Byzantium from 1081 to 1185. During Romanus' reign the Comneni had supported him against the Doukai. But this changed in 1081 for one very important reason – Alexius Comnenus married into the Doukas family, thereby uniting the two for political purposes. He did this to secure the throne when, unable to take Constantinople by storm, he relied on Caesar John's (the same Caesar John who ousted Romanus) support to gain entry to Constantinople to depose the Emperor Botaneiates.[45] Caesar John provided this in return for Alexius' agreement to marry his granddaughter, Eirene, who was none other than the daughter of Andronicus Doukas, the traitor of Manzikert.[46]

However, the price paid by the Comneni was to become complicit in the Doukai propaganda against Romanus. The most important historical works of the twelfth century were written by the Comneni, in particular, *The Alexiad* of Anna Comnena and *The History* by Nicephorus Bryennius (her husband), both of which tacitly support Psellus' anti-Romanus views and make no mention of Andronicus' betrayal at Manzikert.

Although it is true that later in the twelfth century, when Comnenian power started to wane, there was something of a revival of Attaleiates' pro-Romanus argument, such as that penned by the twelfth-century Byzantine chronicler, John Zonaras;[47] nevertheless, by then, memories of Manzikert had

---

45    Caesar John bribed the mercenaries guarding the gates of Constantinople to let Alexius' army into the city, as described in the previous chapter.

46    Caesar John's last act was to cement a Comnenus-Doukas marriage alliance since his two sons, Andronicus and Constantine, were both dead, and the dynasty faced political extinction.

47    In his *Extracts of History*, published at some point around the mid-twelfth century.

ceased to have the pressing urgency they did in the eleventh century. The passage of time had done its work of confusing posterity as to what had really happened. The Dreadful Day – as Manzikert was called by the Byzantines – had become a confused myth about a foolhardy Emperor who risked and lost a battle.

## MODERN VIEWS OF ROMANUS AND MANZIKERT

Nearly 1,000 years after the Battle of Manzikert, Psellus' partisan views about Romanus still hold surprising sway over historians. This is largely because Romanus' reign remains under-researched,[48] and Psellus' propaganda against him encourages historians to denigrate his achievements, especially the importance of his vision of restoring the Byzantine army. This has also led to confusion about the true significance of the Battle of Manzikert, with some more modern historians questioning whether the battle really was the turning point in Byzantine history seen by an older generation of historians like George Ostrogorsky and Stephen Runciman. Most prominently, the French historian, Jean-Claude Cheynet, wrote an article nearly forty years ago,[49] suggesting that Manzikert was of limited significance since Romanus' army was not fully destroyed and casualties, by his estimation, might have been as low as ten per cent of the total army.

However, Cheynet's view of the Battle of Manzikert is highly questionable. Without wishing to spend too much time on the

---

48  The last book with a comprehensive assessment of Romanus' reign and the Battle of Manzikert was published in 1981 – *The Dreadful Day* by Alfred Friendly.

49  The article is 'Mantzikert: Un Désastre Militaire?' published in *Byzantion*, Tome L, 1980.

minutiae of academic debate, it seems that Cheynet's evidence is selective, based on brief comments by Attaleiates that he saw some Cappadocians and imperial cavalry fleeing after Romanus was surrounded. However, Cheynet chooses to ignore other statements by both Attaleiates and Psellus suggesting that the bulk of the army was destroyed. Psellus is unequivocal on this point when he says: *"...his [Romanus'] army was scattered. Those who escaped were but a tiny fraction of the whole. Of the majority some were taken captive, the rest massacred."*[xciii] Attaleiates isn't quite so clear-cut on the size of casualties, but leaves us in no doubt that the Byzantine army was routed: *"For what could be more pitiable than the entire imperial army in flight, defeated and chased by inhuman and cruel barbarians..."*[xciv]

While it is true that some of the army escaped from Manzikert, including Andronicus' rearguard and most of the western army (on the left wing), Romanus' new army of Cappadocian, Anatolian and Armenian troops, in the centre and on the right wing, were decisively routed. They must have suffered heavy casualties, perhaps as high as fifty per cent. Assuming that they constituted at least half of the Byzantine army at Manzikert, this would mean that not only was around a quarter of the total army killed, maimed or captured but it was also the best half – i.e. the new Cappadocian regiments that had been the core of Romanus' army in his previous largely successful campaigns.

This view is supported by the evidence that Romanus found it very difficult to raise a large army after Manzikert. Attaleiates is clear on this point, saying that *"...he [Romanus] came across very few soldiers who were refugees from the battle".*[xcv] Indeed, we know that, after Manzikert, Romanus failed to raise enough soldiers to beat Crispin's Franks, who probably numbered only a thousand or two.[50] It is therefore almost certain that the civil war was in fact a pretty small-scale military affair as a result of the carnage at Manzikert.

Cheynet's other main contention is that the civil war that followed Manzikert was more significant than defeat at the battle. This confuses cause and effect. The various civil wars – that between the Doukai and Romanus, as well as the later conflict between the Doukai and Botaneiates, and also that between Botaneiates and Alexius Comnenus – all resulted from defeat at Manzikert. This was simply because, after the battle, there was no central Byzantine army strong enough to impose the Emperor's authority over his rebellious subjects. Anatolia was also lost because, after Manzikert, there was no Byzantine army to defend it. Therefore, there seems little doubt that Manzikert was the decisive turning point in Byzantine history, as used to be the conventional view.

However, no matter what view is taken of the significance of Manzikert, Romanus' reign remains neglected and his name dishonoured. This is puzzling because it could be argued that he was one of the most far-sighted Emperors of the eleventh century since he understood that, for the empire to survive, it needed to end its dependence on mercenaries and to revive its strong indigenous army, which had safeguarded it in the tenth and previous centuries. Such a view has never been popular with historians, old or new. However, there is little to argue against it except, of course, the words of Michael Psellus. This now looks like a cover-up that has worked far too effectively and pervasively and for far too long. It is time that Romanus' place in history was reassessed.

---

50   We also know that Bryennius' western army (which had mostly escaped from Manzikert) would not support the Doukai against Romanus since they had taken a vow never to betray him.

## PART III

# The First Crusaders

*Crusader shield*

# 15

# ALEXIUS COMNENUS AND THE CALL TO THE WEST

Alexius Comnenus was one of the most fascinating of all Byzantine Emperors. His daughter described her father thus: *"His dark eyebrows were curved, and beneath them the gaze of his eyes was both terrible and kind. When he came into a gathering and began to speak, you were conscious from the moment he opened his mouth of the fiery eloquence of his tongue..."*[xcvi]

Although Alexius was a man of remarkable energy, determination and resourcefulness, even he could not hold back the rising tide of enemies bursting into the empire from all sides in the 1080s. When he seized the throne in 1081, the empire was on its last legs. Not only were the Turks overrunning Anatolia but he was immediately confronted with a major Norman invasion of the Balkans. Robert Guiscard, the Norman conqueror of Byzantine southern Italy, crossed the Adriatic with a powerful army and laid siege to the Byzantine stronghold of Dyrrachion (Durazzo in modern Albania). Constantinople was his target. Claiming that he wanted to restore the dethroned Emperor Michael VII (who had retired to a monastery), he paraded a monk dressed as Michael VII. Alexius had no choice but to meet him in battle.

In September 1081, Alexius marched west with what was left of the Byzantine army.

This force bore no resemblance to the army that Romanus Diogenes took to Manzikert. The Byzantine units were a low grade feudal force and their military effectiveness was poor. Alexius was dependent on mercenaries – mainly Varangians, Turks and Pechenegs. The battle became something of a re-enactment of the Battle of Hastings in 1066 between the Normans and the Saxons. This was because the core of Alexius' army was a force of Varangians, who were mainly Saxon at this time, consisting of thousands of warriors who had fled Norman England after Hastings. The main contest was a bloody slogging match between Robert Guiscard's Norman knights and infantry with the Varangian guard. The Normans won the day and the Byzantine army was routed with the complete slaughter of the Varangians.

After Alexius' devastating defeat at the Battle of Dyrrachion, many Emperors would either have given up or been overthrown by their own people, but Alexius' hallmarks were his tenacity and political cunning. First, he created a clever diversion against the Normans by persuading the German Emperor, Henry IV, to invade Norman Italy. This caused Robert Guiscard to return to Italy, passing command of the invasion force to his son, Bohemond.[51]

Then, Alexius adopted Turkish tactics against the Normans. He avoided battle, instead wearing them down through skirmishing and ambushes. He managed to slow down Bohemond's advance through modern-day Albania, Macedonia and Greece by strengthening the garrisons in the key towns and cities like Ohrid and Larissa, which held out

---

51   Bohemond would later become the hero of the First Crusade.

in long sieges. The mountainous Macedonian countryside, dotted with Byzantine hilltop forts, also made progress difficult. The Norman offensive petered out in 1083.

But there is no doubt that one of Alexius' greatest gifts was luck. In 1085, the Norman leader, Robert Guiscard, died unexpectedly from fever just as he was preparing a renewed offensive. Back in southern Italy, there was civil war over his succession. The Norman forces withdrew from Albania. Dyrrachion surrendered to the Byzantines. The Norman threat was over, at least for the time being.

However, Alexius' problems were far from over. The Pechenegs had become as big a problem in the Balkans in the mid-1080s as they had been in the 1040s. Those that had settled south of the Danube, within Byzantine territory, revolted and were joined by new tribes coming from the north. In 1087, Alexius was defeated in a pitched battle, and by 1090, the Pechenegs had advanced to the walls of Constantinople itself.

The Pecheneg threat was compounded by the collapse of Alexius' strategy in the east. It is certainly true that in the 1080s, while Alexius fought in the west, all was quiet on the eastern front. Not only was there relative stability with the Turkmen in western Anatolia but Sulayman, the Seljuk emir in control of Anatolia,[52] also supplied Alexius with large numbers of Turkmen mercenaries. Alexius relied on these in his war with the Normans, especially when a force of 7,000 Turkmen helped him to relieve the Norman siege of Larissa in 1083.[xcvii]

However, Alexius had to pay a high price for Sulayman's support. He allowed him to occupy both Nicaea and

---

52    Sulayman had broken away from the Seljuk Empire and formed his own emirate, defeating an army sent to subdue him by Malikshah, who was the Seljuk Sultan and Alp Arslan's son.

Antioch, the two most important cities in the empire after Constantinople. This worked well in the short term. But in the longer term it was disastrous. Although Sulayman remained true to his alliance with Byzantium, when he died in 1085 the treaty broke down. His successor, Abu'l-Kasim, started to raid Byzantine territory. In 1090, he captured Nicomedia, the capital of Bithynia, only fifty miles from Constantinople.

The end of the alliance with the Turks in Nicaea was made doubly difficult by an extraordinary new Turkish threat. This came from a Turkish emir called Chaka, who took the Byzantine city of Smyrna on the western coast of Asia Minor in the late 1080s and proceeded to construct a fleet. As if having the Turkish hordes baying at Constantinople from just across the Bosphorus wasn't bad enough, there was now the threat of a Turkish naval attack on the capital as well. Indeed, Chaka negotiated with the Pechenegs in 1090 for a combined attack on the imperial city. It looked as if the empire had no hope of survival. During the winter of 1090–91, Constantinople was besieged by the Pechenegs while Chaka threatened the city with an attack from the sea. Byzantium was on the brink of annihilation.

But it was saved when a new set of Asiatic Steppe nomads, called the Cumans, appeared from north of the Danube. At first, it seemed that they might join with the Pechenegs against the Byzantines. But Alexius managed to make contact with them and, with lavish gifts, payments of gold, and apparently an extraordinarily extravagant banquet, he persuaded them to join forces with him against the Pechenegs.

At the foot of Mount Levounion, in Thrace, forty miles south of Constantinople, the Pechenegs were decisively defeated by a combined Byzantine and Cuman force on 29 April 1091. The slaughter of the Pechenegs was so devastating that it made a deep impression on the Byzantines. *"An entire people, numbering myriads, was exterminated on a single day,"* Alexius' daughter, Anna Comnena, wrote.[xcviii] In the streets of Constantinople, unable to believe their good luck, the people chanted: *"All because of one day, the Pechenegs never saw the month of May."*[xcix]

However, Chaka's maritime threat continued after the Pechenegs were defeated. He continued to raid the Aegean islands in the 1090s, completely disrupting maritime trade. Records from monasteries in the Aegean islands describe the flight of the monks in the face of the Turkish raiders who were systematically occupying one island after another.[c]

On the other side of the Bosphorus from Constantinople, the position was also desperate. Although Alexius recovered Nicomedia from Abu'l-Kasim in 1091, with the help of 500 knights from Robert of Flanders, it was the last Byzantine bastion against the Turks in Asia Minor. In 1094, it looked as if it might not hold out much longer when an ambitious young emir, Kilij Arslan, seized control of Nicaea from Abu'l-Kasim. He also married a daughter of Chaka's, meaning that Byzantium now faced a concerted Turkish attack from land and sea.

The extent of Byzantine collapse in the east is illustrated by the accounts of the crusaders. When they arrived in Nicomedia in 1097, they found Byzantine soldiers clinging on to their last toehold in Anatolia, surrounded by a blood-spattered battlefield, as they recorded.

*"Oh, how many severed heads and bones of the dead lying on the plains did we then find beyond Nicomedia near that sea! [the Bosphorus beside Constantinople]."*[ci]

## The Plot Against Alexius

Although Alexius had managed to stem the Norman and Pecheneg onslaught in the west, his complete failure to hold back the Turks in the east led to growing dissatisfaction with his rule. In 1094, there was a conspiracy against him. It was led by none other than Romanus Diogenes' surviving son, Nicephorus Diogenes. He was the only person who could claim imperial descent, having been 'born in the purple' when his father was Emperor. In addition, like his father, he was handsome and dashing and inspired respect, as Anna Comnena described.

> *"He was physically strong and boasted that he rivalled the Giants: a broad-chested, blond man, a head taller than others of his generation."*[cii]

Supported by many of the nobility, Nicephorus plotted to kill Alexius. In 1094, when on campaign with the Emperor in the Balkans, he entered the imperial tent with a sword concealed. The Emperor and Empress were soundly asleep, lying side by side. But there was also a young girl beside them, fanning away mosquitoes from the imperial couple. Nicephorus couldn't bring himself to kill the young girl and withdrew. He failed again on another occasion – this time on a hunting party with the Emperor, when he was spotted concealing a sword as he went to bathe. By then it was too late. Nicephorus was arrested and, under torture, he confessed to the plot.

Alexius was nothing if not decisive. He immediately implemented a Stalin-like purge of the army and government. In traditional Byzantine fashion, Nicephorus Diogenes was blinded, like his father Romanus, but apparently survived for several years. Others involved in the coup were also blinded. Many members of the old aristocracy were exiled to monasteries or removed from their positions. Even Alexius' own family weren't spared. His brother, Adrian, who had commanded the western armies and tacitly supported Nicephorus Diogenes' plot, was stripped of his rank and exiled to a monastery.

But Alexius knew that with the Turks just across the Bosphorus and the emir Chaka building up his fleet in the Aegean, Byzantium's survival could be numbered in years, if not months. He had to find help from somewhere – and the only place that he could look to was the West.

## The Call to the West

But a call for help to the West was made difficult by the long history of tension between the Pope in Rome and the Patriarch in Constantinople. The roots of this go back to the earliest days of Christianity when Peter was regarded by Christians as the first Bishop of Rome with primacy over all other Christian churches based on Jesus' description of Peter as "The Rock of My Church". However, Rome's primacy was contested when the Emperor Constantine moved the Roman capital to Constantinople in 330AD, and especially when the Emperor Justinian instituted 'caesaropapism' – i.e. the authority of the Emperor in Constantinople to appoint all bishops – at a time when Rome had been reconquered by the Byzantines. With Byzantine loss of control of Rome, autonomous Bishops of Rome re-established their primacy over the churches in western Europe, calling themselves Popes.

There followed centuries of dispute between Rome and Constantinople, ultimately resulting in the Schism of 1054,

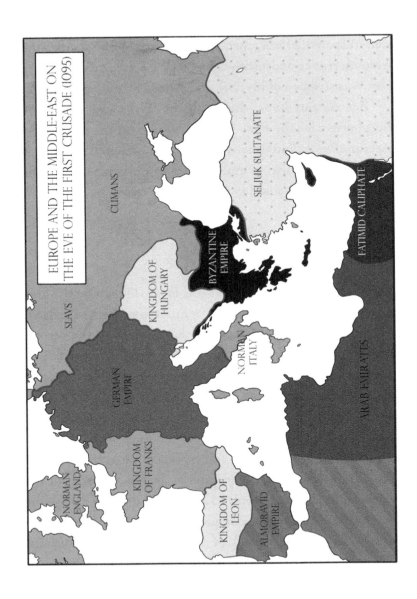

EUROPE AND THE MIDDLE-EAST ON THE EVE OF THE FIRST CRUSADE (1095)

SLAVS

CUMANS

KINGDOM OF HUNGARY

BYZANTINE EMPIRE

SELJUK SULTANATE

FATIMID CALIPHATE

GERMAN EMPIRE

NORMAN ITALY

ARAB EMIRATES

KINGDOM OF FRANKS

NORMAN ENGLAND

KINGDOM OF LEON

ALMORAVID EMPIRE

which was a formal division between the Eastern and Western Churches. The division was purportedly a dispute over doctrine,[53] but in reality it was a power struggle for leadership of the Christian faith. However, the Schism became less acrimonious when both Rome and Constantinople found a common enemy in the Norman adventurers in southern Italy who threatened both papal and Byzantine power.

In 1074, Michael VII's government had proposed an alliance to Pope Gregory VII against the Normans. This marked the first cooperation between the Eastern and Western Churches since the Schism. Sympathy for Byzantium was also growing due to the increasingly difficult passage experienced by pilgrims to Jerusalem. The Turkish control of Anatolia made travel difficult and the fall of Jerusalem to the Seljuks in 1074 was seen as an unwelcome sign of their growing power.

One particular pilgrim became an influential supporter of Byzantium in Western Europe – this was Count Robert of Flanders, who travelled to Jerusalem on pilgrimage in 1089 and witnessed at first hand the collapse of Byzantine rule in Anatolia. Indeed, Alexius cultivated him as an ally, asking him for military assistance. In response, Count Robert sent 500 knights to Alexius who were vital in helping the Byzantines recover Nicomedia in 1091. Robert also helped spread the word of Byzantine collapse throughout Western Europe.

Another device used by Alexius to solicit support for Byzantium was to exploit the growing obsession in the West with holy relics. Byzantium was fortunate enough to have more than its fair share of these relics. The most important

---

53  The main doctrinal issue would seem obscure to most people today. It concerned whether the word *Filioque* – meaning 'and the Son (of God)' in Latin – could be added to the recitation of the Nicene Creed in Mass. This started in the West soon after 800, but was regarded as blasphemous by the Byzantines who believed that the Holy Spirit came only from the Father.

of them was the Holy Cross, said to have been brought to Constantinople in the fourth century by the Emperor Constantine. It seems that Alexius started to distribute pieces of this purported relic, together with other items like the clothing Christ wore, the baskets from the feeding of the five thousand, and any number of bones and relics belonging to the Apostles, to the rich and powerful in the West, including powerful monarchs like Henry IV of Germany (who was an opponent of the Sicilian Normans), and above all to the Pope, who in his turn bestowed them on churches and monasteries as a sign of his own power.

In this way, Alexius cleverly curried favour with the West. But initially his appeals to Pope Gregory VII for military assistance met with little success. This was partly because Gregory VII was overwhelmed with problems in the Western Church itself. However, by the early 1090s, his successor, Pope Urban II, had stabilised the church and was more willing to look at new causes that could extend papal power. Any chance to gain greater authority over Constantinople was particularly interesting to him. Even so, at first nothing came of Alexius' appeals but by 1095, he was truly desperate. He sent envoys to Pope Urban II literally begging for help. A delegation arrived in Piacenza in Italy in March 1095, where Urban was presiding over a church council. They delivered an impassioned plea.

"*An embassy of the Emperor of Constantinople came to the synod and implored his lordship the Pope and all the faithful of Christ to bring assistance against the heathen for the defence of the holy church, which had now been nearly annihilated in that region by the infidels who had conquered as far as the walls of Constantinople*"[ciii]

This time, not only was Urban genuinely shocked and worried by the triumph of the Turks over the Eastern Christians, as he called the Byzantines, but he saw an unmissable opportunity to extend Papal authority over Constantinople. His response to Alexius would shake the world.

# 16

# THE MARCH OF THE CRUSADERS

The First Crusade began on a cold, wintry day. On 27 November 1095, in a field outside the city of Clermont in southern France, Pope Urban II delivered a passionate sermon that set the Christian West alight with crusading fervour. No record of his exact words has survived, but we know that the main subject he spoke of was the need to liberate the Eastern Christians, as he called the Byzantines, from the brutal subjugation of the Turks. Although his exhortation went beyond recovering the land lost to the Seljuks, to reconquering the Holy Land and the sacred city of Jerusalem, lost nearly 500 years ago to the Arabs, the emphasis was first and foremost on saving the Byzantines from rape, pillage and slaughter by the Turks, as this account of his alleged words shows:

*"A race absolutely alien to God has invaded the land of Christians, has reduced the people with sword, rapine and flame... And they cut open the navels of those whom they choose to torment with loathsome death, tear out their most vital organs and tie them to a stake, drag them around and flog them, before killing them as they lie on the ground*

*with all their entrails out. What shall I say of the appalling violation of women, of which it is more evil to speak than to keep silent?"*[civ]

His sermon was the highlight of a grand ecclesiastical council that he had called to reform the corrupt Latin Church. Urban wanted to find a cause to re-establish papal authority in a world that was increasingly questioning the role of the medieval Church. That cause would be a holy war. Urban's words hit home. Within weeks, they became the talk of Europe and unleashed an extraordinary mix of emotions, beliefs and hopes that persuaded well over a hundred thousand men and women to leave their homes for what must have seemed a crazily wild adventure in lands about which the vast majority had no experience or understanding.

One of the most unexpected aspects of the First Crusade was its broad appeal across the whole social spectrum of medieval Europe. It was a genuine people's movement, without the participation of the monarchies of Germany, France and England. In the second half of 1096, thousands of men, women and even whole families, drawn from across Europe, set out for the East. Two entirely separate crusading movements converged on Constantinople: the first was the People's Crusade and the second a huge feudal army led by some of the greatest European nobility. The first to reach Constantinople in the summer of 1096 was the People's Crusade, of which Peter the Hermit was the main leader.

Alexius was appalled at the sight of this when it appeared before the walls of Constantinople. It was the exact opposite of what he had hoped for. Instead of a disciplined military force, such as Robert of Flanders' 500 knights, he looked in horror at a huge rabble of peasants, with a sprinkling of knights.

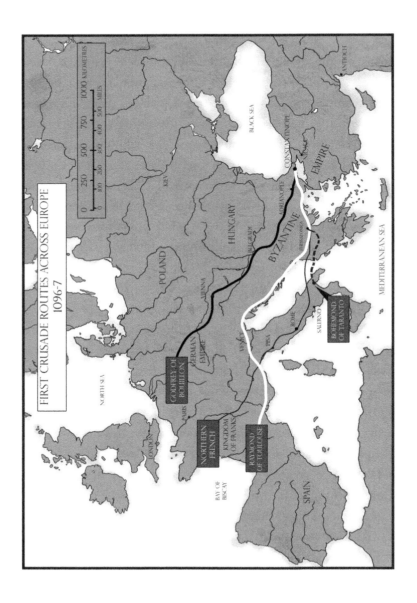

FIRST CRUSADE ROUTES ACROSS EUROPE
1096-7

Inspired by local preachers, such as Peter the Hermit, who had enthusiastically taken up Pope Urban's call for a crusade, this mob is best remembered for the extreme brutality with which it massacred German and French Jews before setting out for Byzantium in what has been called the 'First Holocaust'.

Alexius ferried this rabble across the Bosphorus as quickly as possible. In spite of the People's Crusade having perhaps 1,000 knights and several thousand foot soldiers, when it advanced on the Turkish stronghold of Nicaea, it was annihilated by Kilij Arslan's Turkish warriors. Peppering the mass of peasants with arrows, before charging home with swords and maces, the slaughter was on such a scale that a Frankish observer later recorded that the corpses of these very first crusaders were so numerous that they created: "*I will not say a mighty ridge or hill or peak, but a mountain… so huge was the mass of bones.*"[cv]

The second wave of crusaders was quite different. It consisted of the feudal armies of some of the greatest nobles in Europe. The most important of these were Raymond of Toulouse, Godfrey of Bouillon, Baldwin of Boulogne, Hugh of Vermandois, Robert of Normandy, Robert of Flanders and Stephen of Blois. This overwhelmingly Frankish army was joined by the battle-hardened Normans of southern Italy who were to play a crucial role in the crusade, led by Bohemond of Taranto and Tancred of Hauteville. The whole force is estimated to have numbered at least 80,000 people, of whom over half were knights and foot soldiers, with the rest non-combatants, since some of the crusaders travelled with their wives, families and retainers.

This was exactly the type of force which Alexius had been hoping for although the sheer size of it far exceeded his expectations. Nevertheless, he saw his opportunity and seized it. Organising excellent logistical support for the huge numbers that poured into the western provinces, he showered the Frankish nobility with gifts and required them to swear oaths of allegiance. Impressed by the size and splendour of Constantinople, the Franks and even Byzantium's former Norman enemies, who had been fighting Alexius only ten years earlier, accepted his authority. Overawed by Constantinople, one crusader recorded: *"Oh what a noble and beautiful city is Constantinople! How many monasteries and palaces it contains, constructed with wonderful skill! It would take too long to describe all the wealth that is there of every kind, of gold, of silver, all types of clothes and holy relics…"*[cvi]

The first target was Nicaea. This was Kilij Arslan's capital and had been the third city of Byzantium after Constantinople and Antioch. But the problem was not just Kilij Arslan's Turkmen army but the city walls which were second only to those of Constantinople. Five kilometres long and punctuated with a hundred towers, as well as a double ditch, they were almost impregnable. As one Frank wrote: *"Skilful men had enclosed Nicaea with such lofty walls that the city feared neither the attack of enemies nor the force of any machine"*[cvii]

However, the sheer size of the crusading army impressed the Turks. Kilij Arslan travelled east to gather a force large enough to face the crusaders and, in May 1097, he returned. Advancing out of the hills to the south of Nicaea, thousands of Turkish cavalry poured towards the crusaders. Based on their experience of the People's Crusade and the weak Byzantine forces they had faced, the Turks were fairly contemptuous of the Frankish knights and charged the first group of crusaders they met head-on – Raymond of Toulouse's knights. But the Provençal knights held their ground and when Bohemond's Normans charged the Turks in the flank, they broke and retreated. Although this was not a decisive victory, and Kilij Arslan retreated with the bulk of his forces intact, it marked a new beginning. The crusaders were a force to be reckoned with.

But taking Nicaea was more difficult. The siege dragged on into June. Its walls were impossible to scale, and although the crusaders tried to dig tunnels underneath them, hoping to cause their collapse through sapping operations, these attempts failed. Starving the city into submission seemed to be the only solution. But there was a major obstacle to this. The western edge of the city bordered the great Askanian Lake, allowing the Turks to ferry supplies into the city in small boats. The lake was too large to be patrolled and anyway the crusaders had no boats. The siege looked set to last for many more months. And meanwhile news reached the crusaders that Kilij Arslan was organising a huge Turkmen army, recruited from across the whole of Anatolia, to relieve the city. Some of the crusaders started to wonder whether the crusade would end at Nicaea.

However, Alexius had not been idle. Recovering Nicaea was central to his aim to recover at least part of Anatolia from the Turks, and to achieve this he came up with one of his most resourceful stratagems. This was a plan to haul Byzantine boats twenty miles overland from the coast to the Askanian Lake. This allowed the small Byzantine army that accompanied the great host of crusaders to launch an attack on the unprotected lakeside of the city. Before this, Alexius' general, Manuel Boutoumites, had secretly sent envoys into Nicaea to start negotiations with the Turks, guaranteeing their safety if they surrendered. It should be remembered that the majority of its inhabitants were Greek-speaking Byzantines, who wanted not just to return the city to the empire, but to save themselves from the inevitable pillage of the city and slaughter of at least some of its inhabitants should the crusaders break through the walls.

Therefore, they managed to smuggle Alexius' general, Manuel Boutoumites, into the city with a *chrysobull*,[54] promising the Turkish garrison not only safe passage but even a reward of money if they surrendered the city. The Turks agreed, and he sent the small fleet of Byzantine ships across the lake to the city walls. The Turks surrendered to the Byzantine soldiers disembarking from their ships. Alexius, worried that his secret agreement with the Turks might meet with the crusaders' disapproval, even staged a mock attack on the walls facing the lake where his troops landed. A Byzantine standard was soon raised on these walls, as the crusaders were independently attacking the landward walls, and to the sound of trumpets and horns, the city was proclaimed captured by the Emperor.

The capture of Nicaea was a triumph for Alexius. But for the crusaders, it was only the very beginning of their expedition. Jerusalem still lay over 1,000 miles away, deep within Seljuk Turkish territory. And Kilij Arslan was hurrying towards Nicaea with a large army of Turkmen. The crusaders were about to have to fight a major pitched battle against the Turks if they were to proceed any farther in Anatolia.

Alexius held a council of war with the crusaders. He advised them to march across Anatolia to recapture the other great city of the Byzantine east – Antioch – which was on the route to Jerusalem. Not only would the recapture of Antioch be a huge gain for him, but just as importantly, as the crusaders advanced across Anatolia, they would draw the Turks away

---

54   This was a document signed by the Emperor in gold letters.

from the Eastern Aegean, allowing him to launch his long-awaited offensive to recover the islands and cities on the coast that had fallen to the dangerous emir Chaka, based at Smyrna. Indeed, this strategy was to prove remarkably successful, and Smyrna, Ephesus and all the towns and islands in the Eastern Aegean were recaptured by the Byzantines in the course of 1097–8.

But Alexius made a mistake in underestimating the crusaders' potential. After Nicaea, he didn't want to risk sending troops with them and only despatched one of his most trusted generals, called Taticius,[55] with them to help in choosing the best route and securing provisions. One of the biggest challenges facing the crusaders was logistics, given the sheer size of the crusader army which still numbered over 70,000 people, maybe half of whom were non-combatants. Since such a large force needed to live off the land, it was decided to split it into two. It was just the opportunity the Turks had been waiting for.

All the Normans from both Sicily and France, together with some of the French knights, moved together in one group led by Bohemond, Robert of Normandy and Stephen of Blois, while the main army of Frankish knights led by Godfrey of Bouillon, Robert of Normandy and Robert of Flanders formed a separate column. The two armies agreed to meet at the now disused Byzantine military base at Dorylaion in Phrygia. Little did they know that Turkish scouts were watching their every movement.

Bohemond reached Dorylaion on 30 June and set up camp, waiting for the Franks to join him. He was held in high

---

55   A boyhood friend of Alexius', despite being of Arab or even Turkish parentage, the end of his nose had been cut off, so that he covered his deformity with a gold proboscis.

respect by the crusaders and even the Byzantines were in awe of their erstwhile enemy, as Anna Comnena recorded:

*"Bohemond's appearance was, to put it briefly, unlike that of any other man seen in those days in the Roman world, whether Greek or barbarian. The sight of him inspired admiration, the mention of his name terror…"*

On the morning of 1 July, a few hours after dawn, a huge number of Turkish horsemen came into view. One eyewitness said there were 360,000 of them but this is obviously a wild exaggeration. Nevertheless, the Turkmen army probably approached almost the size of that commanded by Alp Arslan at Manzikert, numbering up to perhaps 30,000. Facing it stood less than half of the crusader army – some 15,000 Norman knights and foot soldiers. Kilij Arslan launched a brutal attack against the Normans as they hurried to form a battle line. One of Bohemond's soldiers recorded that: *"The Turks began, all at once, to howl and gabble and shout, saying with loud voices in their own language some devilish words which I do not understand… screaming like demons."*[cviii]

It was Bohemond's finest hour, as medieval minstrels would sing for centuries to come. He was everywhere organising the defence. The Normans fell back to a nearby stream and Bohemond kept his soldiers in a tight formation around it. He grouped the foot soldiers and knights together, ordering the knights not to break ranks and charge the Turks. Crossbowmen picked off the Turkmen. Behind the mass of heavily armoured knights and infantry, he set up a camp where all the women and children were grouped, tending to the wounded and bringing water from a nearby stream to the soldiers in the front line.

The Normans were battle-hardened veterans and probably the finest soldiers in Europe. They resolutely faced wave after wave of Turkish horsemen. While some of the Turks tried to hack their way through the Norman line, the majority turned round, releasing their arrows and riding off. But the Normans didn't break formation. The dense mass of Norman infantry and knights stood firm while crossbowmen and archers shot the Turkish horsemen down.

For half a day, the Turks surged against the mass of Normans but nowhere could they break their ranks. When a small group broke through into the Norman camp, one crusader recalled the panic of the non-combatants:

> *"The Turks burst into the camp in strength, striking with arrows from their horn bows, killing pilgrim foot soldiers, girls, women, infants and old people, sparing no one on grounds of age. Stunned and terrified by the cruelty of this most hideous killing, girls who were delicate and very nobly born were hastening to get themselves dressed up, offering themselves to the Turks, so that at least, roused and appeased by love of their beauty, the Turks might learn to pity their prisoners."*[cix]

But the Turkish attack was beaten off. In desperation, Bohemond sent messenger after messenger to the second crusader army asking it to come to their rescue. Eventually, as the Turks were preparing for the attack they hoped would break the weary Normans, the French crusaders arrived. A mass of French knights charged the Turks in the flank.

At the same time, the papal legate, Bishop Adhemar of Le Puy, led a group of Provençal knights round the back of the mass of Turkish horsemen. Like most bishops, he came of knightly stock and could understand a battlefield. Raising his sword, he charged into the back of the Turkish army. The Turks, attacked on all sides, broke and fled in panic. Bohemond's Normans surged forward. Even the fast Turkish ponies couldn't get their riders away from the crusaders' swords. The Turks were slaughtered as they fled. Their camp was captured. Kilij Arslan fled, humiliated and defeated, as a Norman soldier recorded: "*The Turks fled very fast to their camp, but they were not allowed to stay there long, so they continued their flight and we pursued them, killing them, for a whole day…*"[cx]

While the crusaders had won a resounding victory, they were impressed with the Turks' courage: "*What man, however experienced and learned, would dare to write of the skill and prowess and courage of the Turks… you could not find stronger or braver or more skilful soldiers.*"[cxi]

The battle of Dorylaion marked a turning point. For the first time, the might of the Seljuk Turks had been stopped in its tracks. The crusaders had come of age.

# 17

# THE SIEGE OF ANTIOCH

As the crusaders marched south from Dorylaion, they entered a wasteland. The Turks retreated before them, poisoning wells and burning trees and crops. It was August and incredibly hot which made their progress even more difficult. But they had one advantage – nowhere would the Turks stand and fight, still in awe of the crusaders' victory at Dorylaion. They fled the ruined Byzantine towns. The crusaders reached Iconium in Cappadocia, and then marched on to Heraclea. There they found themselves confronted by the towering Taurus Mountains which they would need to cross or travel around to reach the plains of Syria. They stopped and asked the Byzantine general, Taticius, who had accompanied them from Nicaea, which route to take.

He advised that there were two – one straight south through dangerously narrow mountain passes, called the Cilician gates, and the other heading northwards through the less dangerous Anti-Taurus Mountains before turning south to Syria. The crusader leaders decided to split the army, with a smaller force heading south, while the bulk of the troops took the easier northern route. By doing this, they would emerge in a pincer movement on the great city of

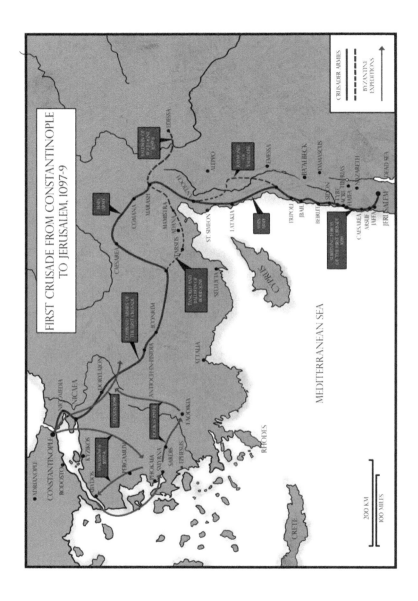

FIRST CRUSADE FROM CONSTANTINOPLE
TO JERUSALEM, 1097–9

CRUSADER ARMIES

BYZANTINE
EXPEDITIONS

MEDITERRANEAN SEA

CYPRUS

RHODES

CRETE

200 KM

100 MILES

ADRIANOPLE
CONSTANTINOPLE
RODOSTO
ABYDOS
KYZIKOS
NICAEA
NIKOMEDIA
PERGAMON
DORYLAEON
PHILOMELION
SMYRNA
FOCIA
SARDIS
EPHESUS
LAODIKEA
ANTIOCH-IN-PISIDIA
IKONIUM
ATTALIA
CAESAREA
COMANA
MARASH
ALBISTAN
MAMISTRA
TARSUS/ADANA
SELEUCIA
ST SIMEON
LATAKIA
EDESSA
ALEPPO
MAMISTRA
TRIPOLI
JBAIL
BEIRUT
SIDON
TYRE
MORE TIBERIAS
NAZARETH
ACRE
CAESAREA
ARSUF
JAFFA
JERUSALEM
DEAD SEA
DAMASCUS
BAALBECK
EMESA

PEOPLE'S CRUSADE
1096

TOGHRIL

Antioch which Taticius said was essential to capture before moving south to Jerusalem.

The crusaders who crossed the Taurus Mountains found it hard going, and just as had happened to Romanus' army returning along the same route from his first campaign in 1068, some plunged to their deaths along the narrow mountain passes. The larger army to the north bypassed the mountains and had an easier time. Finally, the two armies were reunited in front of the great city of Antioch. Their first reaction was one of despair. *"We found the city of Antioch very extensive, fortified with incredible strength and almost impregnable,"* Stephen, Count of Blois, wrote to his wife.[56]

Antioch had previously been the third largest city of the Roman Empire and the second largest in the Byzantine Empire. It had huge fortifications that stretched for five miles with some 400 towers, as well as an imposing citadel. Having fallen to the Turks in 1085, it was now garrisoned by some 5,000 troops under the command of Yaghi Siyan, who owed allegiance to the Seljuk emir Ridwan of Aleppo.

Deciding that the fortifications were too strong for a direct assault, the crusaders settled down to a siege, hoping that the Turks would surrender when their provisions ran out. But as the autumn of 1097 progressed, they found that they were the ones running out of food. Initially, the countryside had provided them with ample sustenance, helped by Byzantine supplies from Cyprus which Taticius organised. But the sheer size of the army meant that it ate the countryside bare.[57] By the end of 1097, the crusaders were starting to starve. According

---

56 This knight's letters home to 'his most sweet and amiable wife, and his dear children' include gruesome details of combat and the beheading of Turks.

57 The crusader army had thousands of horses as well as men and women. Maintaining a single horse requires up to ten gallons of water a day, as well as hay and grazing land.

to one of the main chroniclers, *"The poorer people ate even the hides of animals and the seeds of grain found in manure."*[cxii] But worse was to come. News arrived that the Seljuk emir of Damascus, Duqaq, was advancing with a large army of Turks and Arabs to lift the siege.

Luckily for the crusaders, although Duqaq's army was formidable, it was only the army of a single Seljuk emirate – that of Damascus. The crusaders' greatest advantage by far was that the Seljuk Empire had splintered into a host of largely independent emirates. This had occurred after Malik-Shah's death,[58] when his son Berkyaruq (1092–1105), although nominally the Sultan of Baghdad with authority over both Iran and Iraq (while his brother, Sanjar, ruled the eastern half of the empire extending to modern India), failed to impose his authority over the Syrian emirs in Damascus, Aleppo and Mosul who ruled independently. Therefore, there was no concerted effort by the Seljuk Empire to field a major force against the crusaders, such as Alp Arslan had done at Manzikert against the Byzantines. Indeed, the Seljuk emirs of Syria and Iraq were often in conflict with each other, giving the crusaders the opportunity to pick them off one by one. There is no doubt that this was the single most important reason for the First Crusade's success.

The crusaders had another major advantage: the military genius of Bohemond. Bohemond had learned that the best way of fighting the Turks was to force them into close-quarter combat where the heavy armour of the knights could be used most effectively. He had used this tactic to great effect at Dorylaion, and he used it again against Duqaq's army. When out on a foraging expedition to find food, he and Robert of

---

58    Malik-Shah was Alp Arslan's son and the last Seljuk ruler to rule a truly united Seljuk Empire.

Flanders spotted the advancing Turkish army. Instead of retreating, Bohemond led a blistering charge against the Turks. While there was a confused battle with heavy casualties on both sides, Duqaq decided to retreat and returned to Damascus.

But within days another Seljuk army appeared, this time led by the emir of Aleppo, called Ridwan. A substantial force of crusaders left Antioch to face the Turks, with Bohemond, Robert of Flanders and Stephen of Blois. Once again, it was Bohemond who took the leading role in the battle. Waiting for the Turkish cavalry to fully engage the crusaders, he held his Norman knights back until the Turks had formed a dense mass of horses, unable to use their bows or to turn around and ride off. He then charged with his heavy cavalry and swept through the Turkish ranks. One of Bohemond's men has left a vivid description of the force and bravery of his attack. *"So Bohemond, protected on all sides by the sign of the Cross, charged the Turkish forces, like a lion which has been starving for three or four days, which comes roaring out of its cave thirsting for the blood of cattle."*[cxiii]

Bohemond's charge routed the Turkish army, with the crusaders pursuing them as far as Harim, capturing precious horses and much needed supplies. But although these two victories lifted the crusaders' morale and brought in some additional provisions, there was no sign that Antioch was closer to surrender and the army was still critically short of food. Indeed, the defenders were surviving better than the besieging army, partly due to food being smuggled in and also because the population, unlike the crusader army, had no need to keep thousands of horses fed and watered.

When news arrived that a third, and even larger, Turkish army was on its way, this time led by Kerbogha, the emir of Mosul, and under the instructions of the Seljuk Sultan,

Berkyaruq himself, something had to be done to end the siege quickly. It was again Bohemond who found a solution. And there was a reason for this. It became clear that Bohemond wanted to take Antioch for himself. Although in Constantinople it had been agreed with Alexius that the former cities within the Byzantine Empire would be returned to Byzantine control, Bohemond proposed that, since Alexius had done nothing to help the crusade since the fall of Nicaea, whoever of the crusaders was able to breach the city walls and bring the exhausting siege to an end should be given the city as his own to rule. With Kerbogha bearing down on Antioch, Raymond of Toulouse, the richest and most powerful of the crusaders, together with the other crusader leaders, reluctantly agreed to Bohemond's demands, but on the condition that Antioch would ultimately be returned to Byzantium.

Bohemond made this offer because he was concealing a trump card. This was the contact he had made with an enemy commander responsible for a stretch of the city walls. Called Firouz, this man was probably Armenian, and he spoke Greek as did Bohemond and other Sicilian Normans, making communication easier.[59] He agreed to let the crusaders scale his section of the walls and then open one of the main gates.[60] The plan worked and Bohemond was able to open the Gate of St George and let Robert of Flanders and Godfrey of Bouillon lead their men in. Thereafter, the city was quickly taken, apart from the citadel which remained in Turkish hands. Inevitably, the local Muslim inhabitants were slaughtered, although since the city had been in Byzantine hands only thirteen years

---

59  According to Anna Comnena, Bohemond's Greek was pretty basic and he had a terrible accent.

60  Firouz's motivation has never been made entirely clear; some crusaders said Bohemond had taken his son hostage, others that he had been inspired by God.

before, there were still many Christians, most of whom seem to have been spared. On 3 June 1098, eight months after the siege began, Antioch was finally in crusader hands. The very next day, Kerbogha arrived with his army.

Kerbogha's army was about the same size as Kilij Arslan's had been at the Battle of Dorylaion – probably around 20–30,000 strong – and mainly consisting of Turkmen, supplemented with Arabs. By this time, the crusader army had shrunk to some 20,000 knights and foot soldiers, and was outnumbered. Kerbogha immediately made contact with the Turkish garrison in the citadel which was situated in the city walls and accessible to his army. He launched an attack into the city from the citadel but it was driven back after fierce fighting. Kerbogha then decided to lay siege to the city and starve it into submission. The besiegers became the besieged. But now their food supplies were critically low and they knew they couldn't last long.

It was at this lowest point that the crusaders proved most resourceful. When morale was sinking, and men were fleeing the city at night in despair, Raymond of Toulouse and Bishop Adhemar of Le Puy told the crusaders that a miracle had happened. A peasant from Provence – called Peter Bartholomew – had told them of a dream in which Christ himself had revealed to him the whereabouts of the Roman lance that had been used to pierce his side at the crucifixion. Miraculously, the Holy Lance was discovered in the place indicated in his dream – under the floor of the Church of St Peter in Antioch. Although this was in fact a ruse designed to boost flagging morale, and suspected as such by many,[61] it worked. Brought out and displayed to the crusaders, it gave

---

61   The Holy Lance became a source of intense controversy among the crusaders. Later in the crusade, Peter Bartholomew walked through fire as a test of the veracity of his dream. He died of his burns.

them hope for one more battle. Just as importantly, it was agreed that the commander for the coming battle would be Bohemond. He would not disappoint them.

On 28 June, Bohemond led the majority of the crusader army out of the city in a surprise attack. Since almost all the horses had died or been eaten, Bohemond could no longer launch the fierce cavalry charges that had brought him victory before. Instead, displaying his creative and versatile military talent, he marshalled the crusaders into disciplined infantry ranks and marched them out of the city gates and across the bridge over the Orontes River that flowed in front of the city. The Turks hadn't expected such a move. Kerbogha was playing chess and didn't believe that the crusaders would dream of attacking. The Turkish camp, full of women as well as the possessions of the nomadic Turkmen, was sited in a particularly vulnerable position close to the city. The crusaders' rapid advance threw them into a panic. Without a proper battle plan, the Turkmen leapt on their horses and spurred them towards the crusaders, showering them with arrows. But the crusaders, with the Holy Lance carried in their midst as a standard, surged forward in disciplined ranks led by Bohemond.

Row upon row of crusaders, with the knights fighting as infantry, pushed the Turks back. And as one group of Turks retreated, they crashed into the group behind them. The result was chaos. It was made even worse by the fact that Kerbogha's army was made up of several independent units, some of which had little loyalty to him and fled. The crusaders tramped forward with grim determination, slaughtering whoever was in their way. They captured the Turkish camp, where one crusader grimly recounted: *"When their women were found in the tents, the Franks did nothing evil to them except pierce their bellies with their lances."*[cxiv]

Kerbogha fled back to Mosul. The citadel at Antioch immediately surrendered. Bohemond had led the crusaders to another astonishing victory. Now there was no significant enemy force for hundreds of miles. The path to Jerusalem lay open. But there was one problem – and this time it lay with Bohemond himself.

# 18

# THE ROAD TO JERUSALEM

After defeating Kerbogha, it became clear that Bohemond, the architect of the crusaders' success, had no wish to continue to Jerusalem. Instead, he wanted to remain at Antioch. The truth was that Bohemond was an ambitious opportunist, and the real reason for his joining the crusade was to build a kingdom for himself in Syria, just as his father, Robert Guiscard, had done in southern Italy. Antioch was to be his capital city. To the other crusaders this was tantamount to treachery.

However, for the time being, all of the crusaders were simply exhausted by the protracted siege. On 3 July 1098, the council of the crusader leaders decided to postpone the advance south to Jerusalem until November, to give their troops time to recuperate as well as to avoid the searing heat of the Syrian summer. However, this delay only allowed the infighting to escalate. In particular, relations came to a head between Bohemond and Raymond of Toulouse.

Raymond of Toulouse was in his mid-fifties, elderly by medieval standards, but still fiercely ambitious and the wealthiest and most powerful of the crusaders. He saw himself as the natural leader of the crusade, although so far it had survived without a leader through the surprisingly effective cooperation of the various feudal lords. But now Bohemond's claim that he should be granted Antioch set alight a fierce dispute that looked as if it would break the crusade apart.

The disagreement was over whether Antioch should be returned to Byzantium or not. Bohemond's argument was that the agreement made with Alexius in Constantinople to return Byzantine cities captured by the crusaders to him had been nullified by his apparent abandonment of the crusaders. The other crusaders couldn't deny that there was much truth in Bohemond's claim.

Why had Alexius abandoned the crusaders? He was certainly influenced by several senior crusaders who had themselves abandoned the siege and returned home, most prominently Stephen of Blois. Meeting Alexius on his return journey, Stephen had told him that the crusade was doomed. This seems to have made an impact on Alexius who ordered his general, Taticius, to leave Antioch in the spring of 1098 before Kerbogha's advance on the city. While there is some evidence that Taticius' departure was also prompted by his work organising provisions for the crusaders from Byzantine-controlled Cyprus,[cxv] this was in effect the point when Alexius gave up on the crusaders.

In retrospect, it can be seen that this was a huge mistake. By writing off the crusaders, Alexius missed a golden opportunity to recover Antioch. But it shouldn't be forgotten that he had already benefited from the crusaders' victory at Dorylaion which had allowed the Byzantine army and navy to recover the Aegean islands and the cities along the Eastern Aegean coast, previously controlled by the extremely dangerous Turkish emir Chaka.

The crusaders' acrimonious dispute meant that, in the last months of 1098, it looked as if the First Crusade would disintegrate. Antioch was divided between the crusaders, each lord holding part of the city, with Bohemond commanding the most strategically important part – the citadel. Morale plummeted. Then plague, almost certainly typhoid, broke out in the city, probably due to the large number of hastily buried corpses.

The crusaders started to raid the Syrian towns outside Antioch to obtain supplies. But this didn't reunite them. Indeed, the stand-off between Bohemond and Raymond of Toulouse was extended into the Syrian plain, where the town of Marrat was captured with extreme brutality and the slaughter of its Muslim inhabitants, only to be divided up between the opposing soldiers of Bohemond and Raymond.

With Bohemond intransigent, it was finally Raymond who decided that it would serve his interests best to capture Jerusalem, even if it meant abandoning Antioch to Bohemond. Joined by Robert of Normandy, in January 1099, he marched south. Although Godfrey of Bouillon and Robert of Flanders didn't join him, the initial advance was easy. The reason for this was that, with the fading of Seljuk authority in Syria, many towns to the south of Antioch were ruled by Arab emirs who disliked the Seljuk Turks as much as they did the crusaders, and were not sorry to hear of Kerbogha's defeat. Consequently, the Arab cities of Shaizar, Homs and Tripoli all offered tribute to Raymond rather than face attack. But this changed when Raymond settled down to besiege the coastal fortress of Arqa. Strongly defended, his soldiers couldn't storm its walls.

It looked as if the crusade had stalled yet again. But, while Bohemond stayed resolutely in Antioch, the other crusader leaders, Godfrey of Bouillon and Robert of Flanders, decided to join Raymond. Part of the reason for this was the news that the Seljuks were massing for another attack, although in fact this proved to be false since the Seljuk Sultan, Berkyaruq, was too preoccupied with events in the eastern side of his crumbling empire to care about the crusaders' victories.

But there was a more genuine reason for urgency. News reached the crusaders that the Fatimids had taken Jerusalem from the Seljuks. Being the arch-rivals of the Seljuks, the Fatimids had at first been seen as potential allies. Indeed, a crusader embassy had even been sent to Cairo at Byzantine instigation in 1097,[62] looking for cooperation against the Seljuks in Syria. Now this returned with an intransigent message from the Fatimid leader, al-Afdal. He said that Jerusalem would stay in Fatimid hands. An offer was made that the crusaders could visit the city in peace. But if they wanted to take Jerusalem it was clear that the crusaders would now need to fight a major new enemy – the Fatimid Caliphate.

Leaving Bohemond in Antioch, the rest of the crusaders decided to advance on Jerusalem and take it quickly. With Arqa still holding out, Raymond abandoned the siege. In May 1099 the crusaders marched at speed towards Jerusalem, fearful that Fatimid reinforcements would soon arrive to defend the city. With renewed vigour and confidence caused by the excitement that, after three years, they were finally closing in on their aim of capturing Jerusalem, they skilfully bypassed the Arab strongholds at Tyre and Acre, and on 7 June, Jerusalem finally came into view.

Some crusaders believed that they had reached a potential apocalypse and that if they captured the city, the heavens would open and paradise would descend. But while many wept with joy,

---

62  The Byzantines and Fatimids maintained close diplomatic relations throughout this period, going back to before Manzikert, since both shared a mutual enemy in the Seljuks. However, nothing ever came of their discussions for joint action.

the sight before them was also deeply intimidating for Jerusalem had massive fortifications, nearly four kilometres long.[63] Inside was a sizeable Fatimid garrison, maybe 5,000 strong. The crusader army had shrunk to some 1,300 knights and 12,000 infantry and lacked Bohemond, its most skilful commander. However, the arrival of six Genoese ships at Jaffa with much needed reinforcements provided a welcome boost. With news that a large Fatimid army was within fifteen days' march away, the crusaders knew that they didn't have much time.

They quickly decided on a plan of attack that proved tactically brilliant. Helped by the newly arrived Genoese, who included many carpenters, they rapidly constructed two assault towers, one of which could be dismantled and then reassembled relatively fast. To confuse the defenders, this was moved overnight and reassembled at a different location to the north of the city. At the same time, in the south, the second assault tower was pushed towards the walls with sufficient troops to look as if it was the main attacking force. The deception worked and the majority of the Fatimid defenders rushed to repulse the attack from the south. Meanwhile, the crusaders stepped up their attack with the newly assembled assault tower at the opposite end of the city. A huge battering ram was used to make a breach in the curtain wall and the tower was dragged right up to the main wall.

Although the Fatimids used Greek fire, the crusaders had been warned about this by local Christians and had a good supply of vinegar to put it out.[64] With the wooden sections of the main wall alight, probably due to the Greek fire, and with

---

63  Visitors to the city today can see pretty much what the crusaders saw since the walls to the old city were reconstructed by the Ottomans and follow almost exactly the eleventh-century walls.

64  Greek fire was petrol-based and couldn't be put out with water although vinegar was quite effective.

smoke billowing around him, Ludolf of Tournai established his place in history by being the first crusader to step onto the walls of Jerusalem. He and the other crusaders were able to cut loose some of the hide-covered wattles protecting their assault tower and use them as a bridge onto the city ramparts. Behind Ludolf came a stream of knights, including Godfrey of Bouillon. Once this breach was achieved, the defence of Jerusalem collapsed. Although the Fatimid garrison had succeeded in defeating the diversionary attack to the south, news spread rapidly that the crusaders had taken the northern walls and the defenders abandoned the walls to take up stands in various parts of the city from the Temple Mount to the citadel.

Very few prisoners were taken and the crusaders indulged in an orgy of slaughter that has shocked and horrified future generations. As one eyewitness recounted: *"Some of the pagans were mercifully beheaded, others pierced by arrows plunged from towers, and yet others, tortured for a long time, were burned to death in searing flames. Piles of heads, hands and feet lay in the houses and streets, and men and knights were running to and fro over the corpses."*[cxvi]

The crusaders showed a disturbing mix of emotions in the sack of Jerusalem: bloodlust, greed and then piety. After they had slaughtered almost the entire Muslim community, many of the poorer crusaders – foot soldiers and squires – cut open the corpses, searching for jewels swallowed by their unlucky victims. Then, still covered in blood, the crusader leaders gathered to worship in the Church of the Holy Sepulchre, the church containing the two holiest sites in the Christian religion: the site of Christ's crucifixion at a place known as 'Calvary' or 'Golgotha', as well as his empty tomb where he is said to have been buried and resurrected.

The Church of the Holy Sepulchre still stands today, much the same as it was when the crusaders entered it nearly 1,000 years ago.[65] Perhaps ironically, the original Roman church had been restored by the Byzantines at huge expense in 1048, as part of a growing rapprochement with the Fatimids.

While the streets of Jerusalem ran red with blood, one medieval chronicler has left us with an insight into the conflicting emotions that drove the crusaders. He describes the humility and piety shown by Godfrey of Bouillon. Abstaining from the slaughter that raged in the city, and taking only three of his men, he took off his armour and his shoes and went barefoot outside the city walls so that he could enter the city in humility through the gate that looks out on the Mount of Olives. Continuing barefoot and without any weapons, he walked into the Church of the Holy Sepulchre, where he cried and prayed and gave thanks to God for being granted his greatest wish – to see the Sepulchre of Jesus Christ.

The First Crusade had achieved its objective. But there was one more battle to be fought. For a large Fatimid army, maybe 20,000 strong, was marching on the city.

---

65    Although the crusaders made later additions and its dome was rebuilt in the nineteenth century.

# 19

# THE FINAL ENEMY

With little time to lose, Godfrey of Bouillon was elected leader of the crusaders. So as not to offend the democratic spirit of the crusade, he rejected the grand title of King of Jerusalem and adopted the more humble one of 'Advocate of the Holy Sepulchre'. With the Fatimids nearing the city, the crusader leaders decided not to wait for them in Jerusalem but to march out to meet them in pitched battle. This was a brave decision since, with perhaps only some 1,200 knights and 9,000 infantry still capable of combat, they were outnumbered two to one.

But the Fatimid army was also different from the Turkish armies they had previously encountered. Predominantly Egyptian and Arab, it had a large number of Egyptian infantry who were levies of doubtful quality. More formidable were the Ghulam cavalry who formed a standard part of medieval Muslim armies, together with the Berber and Bedouin tribesmen, and an entirely new type of enemy for the crusaders in the form of Ethiopian infantry, wielding huge war flails – metal spikes on long chains – capable of bringing down both horse and rider. The crusaders knew that if they were defeated, Jerusalem would fall back into Muslim hands. It was a do or die moment – as so many had been in the history of the First Crusade.

On 12 August, the two armies met outside the Fatimid-held port of Ascalon. The sources differ in their accounts of the battle, but most say that the crusaders launched a surprise attack on the Egyptian army. Attacking at dawn, they arranged themselves in a line of battle, with Godfrey on the left wing while the centre was packed with Norman and Frankish knights, the élite of the army, led by Robert of Normandy, Robert of Flanders and Tancred of Hauteville, Bohemond's nephew. As the sun glinted on the horizon, they advanced towards the Fatimid army and broke into a gallop, spears and lances raised.

Al-Afdal was not expecting an attack. Knowing that he outnumbered the crusaders, his focus was on laying siege to Jerusalem and he was more preoccupied with the construction of siege engines than how to face the crusaders in a pitched battle. Because of this, on that morning, his army had failed to post sufficient scouts to warn of the approaching enemy. As the army of Egyptians, Arabs and Ethiopians began to stir, waking up to go about their morning chores, they heard the sound of hooves pounding the ground in the distance. Suddenly, they realised that a host of horsemen was galloping straight towards them. There was panic. Men shouted and screamed at each other. The Egyptian camp erupted into an ants' nest of activity. The Arabs and Ghulams rushed to their horses and the Egyptian infantry grabbed their weapons. Meanwhile, the sound of hooves grew louder and louder.

Quickening their pace, the crusaders broke into a charge. Many were still living on the adrenalin rush of religious fervour, convinced that the capture of Jerusalem would bring an apocalypse and the defeat of the infidel throughout the world. Their confidence knew no bounds as they charged towards the Egyptian army in the early morning sun.

Al-Afdal was still in a state of shock that his army was under attack. He surrounded himself with his heavy Ghulam cavalry and retreated to the rear of the camp, ordering the Egyptian levies to form a battle-line with the Ethiopians and Bedouin tribesmen. There were no defences to the Egyptian camp, no palisades or moats or tripwires. Instead, the ground lay wide open and the Fatimid army waited for the crusader storm to hit them. Yelling their battle cries, the Normans and Franks dug spurs into their horses' flanks to deliver the most powerful cavalry charge known in the medieval world. The crusaders crashed straight into the mass of infantry. The Egyptians' wicker shields splintered under the blows of iron swords. Egyptians, Arabs and Ethiopians were knocked aside, struck down with swords or spitted on spears like wild boar. The iron-clad Normans rode in amongst the tumult of men, slashing and hacking with their swords. Behind them came the Christian foot soldiers, running after the knights, ready to finish off the survivors.

It was then that Robert of Normandy found a place in the minstrels' tales. Robert was the eldest son of King William the Conqueror, and so far had proved a failure in life. Bequeathed Normandy by his father, while his brother, William II, ruled England, he had been ousted by his brother and left Normandy in disgrace. When he heard of the First Crusade he turned to it to find a new purpose to his life. Held in low regard by his peers, it was at the Battle of Ascalon that he earned his redemption.

Having been at the forefront of the crusader onslaught, Robert saw a tall pole gleaming in the centre of the Egyptian camp, surrounded by Ghulam cavalry. Something told him that it must be al-Afdal's standard, and he called the Normans to charge the Ghulams surrounding it. In a frenzy, the Normans fell upon the Ghulams, and Robert dealt the standard-bearer a crunching blow with his sword. As the man fell, Robert grabbed the standard – a tall solid silver pole with a golden apple at its top – and cried out that God had delivered victory.

Seeing al-Afdal's standard in crusader hands, panic seized the entire Egyptian army. It disintegrated with many running to the sea, pursued by Raymond of Toulouse, where they couldn't escape and drowned. Others tried to flee to the safety of the fortress at Ascalon but were caught in its narrow entrance by the sheer weight of numbers. As one crusader grimly commented: "...*our men cut them to pieces as one slaughters cattle for the meat market*[cxvii] Al-Afdal himself just succeeded in escaping into the fortress at Ascalon and managed to return to Egypt. But he was horrified at the scale of his defeat and the destruction of his army.

This was the last battle of the First Crusade and one of its greatest victories. The crusaders had proved invincible. They had shattered Seljuk and Fatimid armies, almost always numerically superior. Although in later centuries, their brutality would attract opprobrium, in their own age they were the greatest of all heroes. Just as Homer's Iliad held audiences spellbound over innumerable evenings in the ancient world, so medieval listeners never tired of hearing of the bravery of Bohemond and the piety of Godfrey of Bouillon. The story of the First Crusade became a legend, recounted in rapture from the campfires of peasants to the castles of kings.

# CONCLUSION

# THE STREAM OF TIME

" The stream of time, irresistible, ever-moving, carries off and bears away all things... both deeds of no account and deeds which are mighty and worthy of commemoration..."[cxviii] So wrote Anna Comnena in the first lines of *The Alexiad*, one of the greatest literary masterpieces of the Middle Ages.[66] Her words convey a sense of uneasiness with the world of the late eleventh century. And well they might. For the scale of conflict between 1068 and 1099 was unparalleled for its time. Not since the fall of the Western Roman Empire in the fifth century or the rise of Islam in the sixth had such an intense conflict been fought over so wide an area. Its like would not be repeated until the Napoleonic Wars and the First World War. The changes wrought in these years were profound. Byzantium was not destroyed but it was broken as a great power. The foundations of modern-day Turkey were laid. But most important of all was the creation of a conflict between Islam and Western Europe, the echoes of which can still be heard today.

---

66 Anna Comnena's *Alexiad* is testimony to the much greater cultural sophistication of Byzantium compared to Western Europe in the eleventh-century.

For nearly a century after the First Crusade, the Franks controlled the Holy Land. There were five crusader states, headed by the Kingdom of Jerusalem, and referred to collectively as 'Outremer'.[67] In the early decades of the twelfth century, the lack of a united Islamic opposition continued to favour them. The Seljuk Empire was shrinking, beset with problems in its eastern territories, and there was no wish to mount a major campaign against the crusaders, such as Alp Arslan had done against the Byzantines. The Egyptian Fatimids didn't cooperate with the largely independent Seljuk emirs in Damascus, Aleppo and Mosul so that the crusaders could still pick them off relatively easily one by one. This allowed the crusader states to flourish in the decades after the capture of Jerusalem.

For Byzantium, the position was less rosy. Although it was saved by the First Crusade, its recovery was certainly not a restoration to what it had been before the Battle of Manzikert. The new front line with the Turks was 500 miles west of Manzikert and the Anatolian heartland of the empire was lost for ever. Cappadocia became home to Turkish tribes, whose settlements paved the way for the Islamisation of one of Christianity's original core geographies. Most important of all, defeat at Manzikert drove the last nail into the coffin of its centuries-old professional army. Thereafter, it became almost entirely reliant on mercenary troops and ceased to be a military power of any real significance.

Byzantine weakness was compounded by a failure to maintain good relations with the newly created crusader states. Alexius Comnenus' biggest mistake was to underestimate the potential success of the First Crusade. Not surprisingly, he

---

67   The French for 'overseas'.

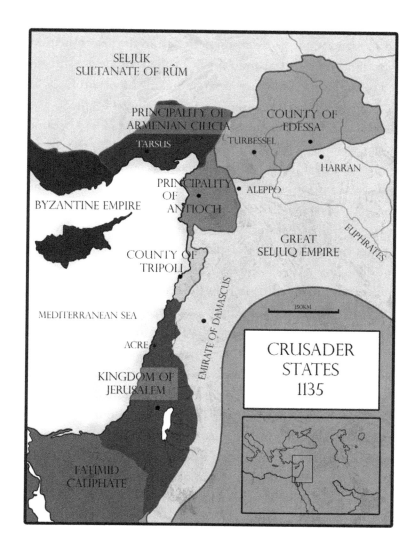

SELJUK
SULTANATE OF RÛM

PRINCIPALITY OF
ARMENIAN CILICIA

COUNTY OF
EDESSA

TARSUS

TURBESSEL

HARRAN

BYZANTINE EMPIRE

PRINCIPALITY
OF
ANTIOCH

ALEPPO

EUPHRATES

COUNTY OF
TRIPOLI

GREAT
SELJUQ EMPIRE

MEDITERRANEAN SEA

EMIRATE OF DAMASCUS

150 KM

ACRE

KINGDOM OF
JERUSALEM

CRUSADER
STATES
1135

FATIMID
CALIPHATE

had no idea that it would achieve its objective and result in the creation of a powerful Frankish presence in the Levant. While there is no doubt that he was responsible for initiating the crusade and dealt with its leaders very skilfully to begin with, for example by securing oaths of loyalty from them in Constantinople, his abandonment of the crusade at Antioch led to the rise of a movement targeting him as a traitor.

Led by Bohemond, this anti-Byzantine movement was propagated by accounts of the First Crusade that became widespread reading in the West.[68] In particular, the *Gesta Francorum* (the Deeds of the Franks), recounted by a knight in Bohemond's army to a cleric who wrote it in Latin, became the main account of the First Crusade. It was poisonous in its portrayal of Alexius and spread false stories of Alexius' connivance with the Turks, such as his supposed delight with the slaughter of the People's Crusade, sparing the Turks at Nicaea, and then failing to help the crusaders at Antioch.

Growing pressure on the crusader states led to further alienation between them and the Byzantines. When Edessa fell to resurgent Islamic forces in 1144,[69] the response from the west was for another great crusade – the Second Crusade. Led by the two most powerful monarchs in Europe, the German Emperor, Conrad III, and the French King, Louis VII, their armies struggled to make it through Anatolia, suffering heavy casualties at the hands of the Turks, and when they reached Outremer, they only managed to launch an attack on Damascus which failed miserably. After this they returned

---

68  Widespread retelling is a more accurate description given that almost all people in the eleventh and twelfth centuries in Western Europe were illiterate except for clerics.

69  These belonged to the emir of Mosul, Imad ad-Din Zengi, who took control of Aleppo as well as Mosul, and presented the crusaders with their most dangerous threat up to this point.

home, the whole expedition deeply disappointing compared with the success of the First Crusade.

One of the consequences of the failure of the Second Crusade was a hardening of opinion against the Byzantines. The French King, Louis VII, found Byzantine forces in Anatolia unwilling to help his troops, and on his return home, looking for a convenient scapegoat, he blamed the failure of the crusade on the Byzantines, even claiming that Byzantium should be attacked first in order to establish a reliable link with Outremer. His words were ominous indeed.

Outremer's decline accelerated the division between Byzantium and the West. This became critical when Saladin finally succeeded in uniting Egypt and Syria against the crusaders and defeated King Guy of Jerusalem at the pivotal Battle of Hattin in 1187. The bulk of the crusader forces were killed or captured. Outremer never recovered from this defeat. Saladin's troops poured into Palestine and Jerusalem was captured after a five-day siege.[70] The Byzantines showed little sympathy. The Emperor Isaac Angelus even sent a letter of congratulation to Saladin and requested that the Holy Places in Jerusalem be restored to Greek Orthodox control. The request was granted.

The response to the fall of Jerusalem from the West was one of outrage and desperation. Pope Urban III is said to have died of shock. His successor, Pope Gregory VIII, issued a call for arms that was to be later known as the Third Crusade. The story of this expedition has passed firmly into English folklore since it was led by King Richard I of England, the 'Lionheart', accompanied for a short time by the French King

---

70  In contrast to the brutal massacre of Muslims in the First Crusade, Saladin allowed the Christian inhabitants to leave unharmed if they paid a ransom of $50 per person in today's money. Most did.

Philip II. Although the German Emperor, Frederick I, also joined the crusade, he was drowned in the Saleph River in Anatolia, leaving Richard and Philip to fight alone. Landing at Acre in 1191, where King Guy of Jerusalem was desperately holding out against Saladin, they pushed back Saladin's forces and raised the siege. Although Richard and Philip quarrelled so that Philip (who was also ill with dysentery) returned to France, Richard marched out of Acre and defeated Saladin in a pitched battle at Arsuf.

But he didn't recapture Jerusalem, although he advanced to within a day's march of the city. Judging that his army wasn't strong enough to take the city, he made a five-year peace treaty with Saladin on condition that Catholics would be allowed to enter Jerusalem on pilgrimage. Richard and Saladin are said to have had great respect for each other, although they never actually met.[71]

Richard saved Outremer from complete destruction. Not only did he defeat Saladin but he also secured the coastal ports of Acre, Tripoli and Jaffa. En route to the Holy Land, he had also captured Cyprus from the Byzantines, a further sign of the decline in relations with Byzantium but a useful asset for Outremer since the island provided a secure base from which to supply the coastal cities. Nevertheless, Jerusalem was firmly back in Muslim hands, and Pope Innocent III began preaching for a new crusade to recover the city.

Yet sentiment was now almost as hostile towards the Byzantines as it was against the Muslims, and in 1204, Venice contrived to redirect the Fourth Crusade away from Egypt towards Constantinople. An army of Franks, transported

---

71  One famous story is that when Saladin heard Richard's horse had been killed in battle, he sent him two fresh horses, with a groom leading them to the crusader camp.

in Venetian ships, stormed the city's sea walls from its most vulnerable side – the Golden Horn – having broken through the great chain that had blocked this narrow isthmus for centuries. The city was then subjected to three days of terror. Although its inhabitants were Christian, the crusaders showed little mercy. They indulged in an orgy of rape, slaughter and pillage. The great cathedral of Hagia Sophia was ransacked. The Orthodox priests were humiliated, if not actually killed. A prostitute was made to sit on the Patriarch's throne. Constantinople had never been subjected to this kind of destruction before. It was the only city to have survived intact from the ancient world, and now its magnificent treasures were looted. The Venetians delighted in taking as many of them back to Venice as they could. The Fourth Crusade destroyed Byzantium just as the First Crusade had saved it.

After the catastrophe of 1204, what was left of the Byzantine ruling class set up three successor states: Trebizond in the east, Epirus in the south, and the strongest, Nicaea, close to Constantinople, became the de facto Byzantine government in exile. Byzantium had not been completely destroyed, and indeed it would even recover Constantinople in 1261, but it was no longer an empire and no longer of much significance. It would struggle on for nearly two hundred years as a city state until the Ottoman Turks finally put it out of its misery in 1453, when their cannons breached the city's ancient walls. The Turkish conquest of Byzantium, begun nearly four hundred years earlier on the battlefield of Manzikert, finally reached its long-awaited conclusion.

But the gift of hindsight can be dangerous. It is all too easy to suppose that Byzantium was doomed at Manzikert, and that the First Crusade was bound to succeed. In fact, the exact opposite is true. The First Crusade was a wildly unlikely success, only made possible by the fragmentation of the Seljuk Empire, the unity of purpose of the crusaders and the military genius of Bohemond. Equally, Romanus Diogenes' epic struggle to stem the Seljuk onslaught has been largely forgotten. In particular, the Battle of Manzikert is clouded with misunderstanding caused by the diatribes of Michael Psellus.

For the Battle of Manzikert should not have ended in defeat. The neglected commentary of Michael Attaleiates provides compelling evidence that Romanus' attempt to revive the Byzantine army was a serious undertaking. Although the army that he marched to Manzikert wasn't the deadly fighting machine of tenth-century Byzantium, its newly trained Cappadocian regiments still massed in disciplined ranks that filled their enemies with fear.

Such, at any rate, was the view of the Turks. Alp Arslan's offer of peace on the eve of battle was prompted by fear of the Byzantine army, not something, for example, felt by Kilij Arslan when he faced the crusaders at the Battle of Dorylaion. So, why did Dorylaion end in victory and Manzikert in defeat? The answer is that the armies of the First Crusade were united while the Byzantines were divided. Romanus Diogenes was brutally betrayed on the battle-field by Andronicus Doukas in a few minutes that changed the course of history. But this was far from inevitable. Had Romanus Diogenes had the foresight to imprison or exile the Doukai, he could have been the hero who saved Byzantium. And the stream of time would have flowed in a new direction.

# ACKNOWLEDGEMENTS

Three Byzantine historians have particularly influenced this book.[72] First, Speros Vryonis, whose seminal book, *The Decline of Medieval Hellenism in Asia Minor*, although written nearly fifty years ago, still paints, to my mind, the most authoritative picture of the conquest of Anatolia by the Turks.

Second, Peter Frankopan's more recent *The First Crusade: The Call from the East* has significantly changed our understanding of the First Crusade by showing that Byzantium's appeal to the West in 1095 was made from a position of weakness rather than strength, as misleadingly depicted in the main contemporary source.[73] This has reinforced the importance of Byzantine defeat at Manzikert as a cause for the First Crusade.

Third, this book could not have been written without the recent translation of Michael Attaleiates' *The History* into English in 2012 by Dimitris Krallis and Anthony Kaldellis. In addition, Krallis' fascinating account of the dual lives of Michael Attaleiates and Michael Psellus, in his book *Michael Attaleiates and the Politics of Imperial Decline in Eleventh-Century Byzantium*, brings essential background and colour to

---

72  Although none of them were consulted on the views expressed in this book which are entirely my own.
73  *The Alexiad* by Anna Comnena.

these two figures in the complex politics of eleventh-century Byzantium.

Finally, I want to thank my late parents – my father, George Holmes, formerly Chichele Professor of Medieval History at Oxford, who shared my love of history but encouraged me to find my own interests rather than his, and to my recently deceased mother who provided so much encouragement. This book is dedicated in their memory. But my greatest thanks of all go to my wonderful wife and children, not least for putting up with so many visits on our holidays to dusty ancient ruins in Greece, Turkey and across the Mediterranean.

# CHRONOLOGY OF THE BYZANTINE EMPIRE

*(With emphasis on eleventh century)*

| | |
|---|---|
| 330 | Emperor Constantine inaugurates Constantinople as the New Rome |
| 406 | Beginning of the fall of the Western Roman Empire |
| 410 | Alaric the Visigoth sacks Rome |
| 527 | Coronation of Emperor Justinian (527–65), who leads a revival of the Eastern Roman Empire (subsequently called Byzantine by historians) |
| 532–7 | Construction of Hagia Sophia in Constantinople |
| 533–40 | Byzantine re-conquest of North Africa and Italy; Vandals and Goths defeated |
| 603–28 | Devastating war with Persia which Byzantium wins but at great cost |
| 632 | Death of Prophet Muhammed. Birth of Islam as a new religion |
| 636–40 | Muslim Arabs begin a war of conquest. They defeat the Byzantines at the Battle of Yarmuk and conquer the Levant and Egypt, then spreading west to Spain and east to India |
| 717–18 | Siege of Constantinople by the Arabs. Against all expectations the Byzantine Empire survives the |

| | |
|---|---|
| | Arab onslaught and clings onto western Anatolia and the Aegean region |
| 800 | Coronation of Charlemagne in Rome as Emperor in the West |
| 867 | Emperor Basil I starts the Macedonian dynasty which sees a recovery in Byzantine fortunes |
| 959–76 | Emperors Nicephorus Phocas and John Tzimiskes, members of the Cappadocian military aristocracy, lead a revitalised Byzantine army. They embark on a war of conquest, taking Crete, Cilicia and northern Syria from the Abbasid Caliphate, and advancing close to Jerusalem (although they do not capture the city) |
| 1022 | Byzantine annexation of eastern Armenia (Vaspurakan) |
| 1031 | Byzantine occupation of Edessa |
| 1043 | Russian attack on Constantinople defeated |
| 1040s–60s | Byzantine Empire subjected to attacks by Asiatic Steppe nomads: Pechenegs in the West and Seljuk Turks in the East |
| 1054 | Schism with Papacy |
| 1061 | Normans start to conquer Sicily |
| 1064 | Seljuk Turks occupy Armenia |
| 1067 | Seljuk sack of Caesarea |
| 1068 | Romanus IV Diogenes crowned Emperor and undertakes his first campaign with the capture of Hierapolis in Syria. Neocaesarea and Amorium sacked by Turkish raiders |
| 1069 | Romanus' second campaign is inconclusive. Turks sack Iconium |
| 1070 | Manuel Comnenus defeated by Turks. Chonae sacked by Turkish raiders. Manzikert taken by Alp Arslan |

| | |
|---|---|
| 1071 | Romanus recaptures Manzikert but is defeated by Alp Arslan at the Battle of Manzikert. Pivotal moment for regular Byzantine army which is almost entirely destroyed. Thereafter, Byzantium dependent on mercenaries. Italy lost to Normans |
| 1072–81 | Loss of Anatolia to Turks. Byzantine Empire dissolves into chaos due to civil wars |
| 1081–94 | Accession of Emperor Alexius Comnenus. First years spent fighting Normans and Pechenegs who are defeated by Alexius. Complete loss of Anatolia to Turks with Turkish occupation of Nicaea and Antioch |
| 1095 | Constantinople under dire threat from Turks on land (Kilij Arslan) and sea (Chaka). Alexius appeals to Pope Urban II to save Byzantium |
| 1097 | First Crusade reaches Constantinople. Nicaea recaptured from Turks who are decisively defeated at the Battle of Dorylaion |
| 1098 | Antioch falls to crusaders |
| 1099 | Jerusalem falls to crusaders. Establishment of crusader kingdoms in the Levant |
| 1147–49 | Second Crusade |
| 1176 | Byzantines defeated by Turks at the Battle of Myriokephalon |
| 1187 | Saladin captures Jerusalem |
| 1189–92 | Third Crusade |
| 1204 | Sack of Constantinople by the Fourth Crusade |
| 1453 | Fall of Constantinople to the Ottoman Turks and the official end of the Byzantine Empire, although Byzantium had been of little significance since 1204. |

# LIST OF RULERS

## GREAT SELJUK SULTANS
## (RULING OVER ALL SELJUK TERRITORIES)

| | |
|---|---|
| 1038–63 | Tughril (western Seljuk territories) |
| 1038–59 | Chaghri (eastern Seljuk territories) |
| 1063–73 | Alp Arslan (all Seljuk territories) |
| 1073–92 | Malikshah |
| 1092–1105 | Berkyaruq |

## SELJUK SULTANS OF RUM
## (RULING THE FORMER BYZANTINE ANATOLIA)

| | |
|---|---|
| 1077–86 | Suleiman I |
| 1092–1107 | Kilij Arslan I |
| 1107–16 | Malikshah |
| 1116–56 | Masud I |

# Concise Bibliography

## Primary Sources

Albert of Aachen, *History of the Journey to Jerusalem* (translated by Susan B Edgington) (Routledge, 2016)

Anonymous, *Three Byzantine Military Treatises* (translated by George T Dennis) (Dumbarton Oaks, 1985)

Attaleiates, Michael, *The History* (translated by Anthony Kaldellis and Dimitris Krallis) (Dumbarton Oaks, 2012)

Comnena, Anna, *The Alexiad* (translated by ERA Sewter) (Penguin, 1969)

Fulcher of Chartres, *A History of the Expedition to Jerusalem* (translated by Frances Rita Ryan) (University of Tennessee Press, 1973)

*Gesta Francorum (aka The Deeds of the Franks and the other Pilgrims to Jerusalem)* (edited by Rosalind Hill) (Oxford, 1962)

Ibn al-Athir, *The Annals of the Saljuq Turks*, (translated by DS Richards) (Routledge, 2002)

Komnene, Anna, *The Alexiad* (translated by ERA Sewter and revised by Peter Frankopan) (Penguin, 2009)

Leo VI, *The Taktika* (translated by George T Dennis) (Dumbarton Oaks, 2010)

Phokas, Nikephoros, *Praecepta Militaria*, (translated by Eric McGeer) (Dumbarton Oaks, 1995)

Psellus, *Michael, Fourteen Byzantine Rulers: The Chronographia of Michael Psellus* (translated by ERA Sewter) (Penguin edition reprint, 2011)

Skylitzes, John, *A Synopsis of Byzantine History 811-1057* (translated by John Wortley) (Cambridge, 2010)

# Secondary Sources

## Byzantines – General Histories

Cameron, Averil, *The Byzantines* (Blackwell, 2006)

Herrin, Judith, *Byzantium: The Surprising Life of a Medieval Empire* (Allen Lane 2007)

Mango, Cyril, *The Oxford History of Byzantium* (Oxford, 2002)

Norwich, John Julius, *Byzantium* (3 volumes) (Penguin, 1988)

Ostrogorsky, George, *History of the Byzantine State* (Blackwell Oxford, 1968)

Sarris, Peter, *Byzantium: A Very Short Introduction* (Oxford, 2015)

Vasiliev, AA, *History of the Byzantine Empire* (Wisconsin, 1952)

## Byzantines – Focus on Eleventh Century and Related Periods

Angold, Michael, *The Byzantine Empire 1025-1204: A Political History* (Longman, 1997)

Blondal, Sigfus, *The Varangians of Byzantium* (Cambridge, 1978)

Cahen, Claude, *La Campagne de Manzikert d'apres des sources Musselmanes* (*Byzantion* Vol. 9, 1934, pp.613–42)

Cheynet, Jean-Claude, *Mantzikert: Un Désastre Militaire?* (*Byzantion*, Tome L, 1980)

Friendly, Alfred, *The Dreadful Day: The Battle of Manzikert 1071* (Hutchinson, 1981)

Haldon, John, *The Byzantine Wars* (Tempus, 2001)

Haldon, John, *Warfare, State and Society in the Byzantine World 565-1204* (Routledge, 2003)

Harvey, Alan, *Economic Expansion in the Byzantine Empire, 900-1200* (Cambridge, 1989)

Holmes, Catherine, *Basil II and the Governance of Empire (976-1025)* (Oxford, 2005)

Kaldellis, Anthony, *The Byzantine Republic* (Harvard, 2015)

Krallis, Dimitris, *Michael Attaleiates and the Politics of Imperial Decline in Eleventh-Century Byzantium* (Arizona Center for Medieval and Renaissance Studies 2012)

Laiou, Angeliki and Morrisson, Cécile, *The Byzantine Economy* (Cambridge, 2007)

Neville, Leonora, *Authority in Byzantine Provincial Society, 950-1100* (Cambridge, 2004)

Neville, Leonora, *Heroes and Romans in Twelfth-Century Byzantium* (Cambridge, 2012)

Neville, Leonora, Anna Komnene: *The Life and Work of a Medieval Historian* (Oxford, 2016)

McGeer, Eric, *Sowing the Dragon's Teeth: Byzantine Warfare in the Tenth Century* (Dumbarton Oaks, 1995)

Treadgold, Warren, *Byzantium and Its Army* (Stanford, 1995)

Vryonis, Speros Jr., *The Decline of Medieval Hellenism in Asia Minor and the Process of Islamization from the Eleventh through the Fifteenth Century* (University of California, 1971)

Wilson, NG, *Scholars of Byzantium* (Duckworth, 1983)

## Seljuk Turks

Cahen, Claude, *Pre-Ottoman Turkey* (Sidgwick and Jackson, 1968)

Hillenbrand, Carole, *Turkish Myth and Muslim Symbol: The Battle of Manzikert* (Edinburgh, 2007)

Peacock, ACS, *Early Seljuq History* (Routledge, 2010)

Peacock, ACS, *The Great Seljuk Empire* (Edinburgh, 2015)

## Crusaders

Asbridge, Thomas, *The First Crusade* (Simon and Schuster, 2004)

Frankopan, Peter, *The First Crusade: The Call from the East* (Vintage, 2013)

Harris, Jonathan, *Byzantium and the Crusades* (Continuum, 2003)

Mayer, Hans Eberhard, *The Crusades* (Oxford, 1972)

Riley-Smith, Jonathan, *The Oxford Illustrated History of the Crusades* (Oxford, 1995)

Runciman, Steven, *A History of the Crusades* (3 volumes) (Oxford, 1951 and Penguin Modern Classics, 2016)

Smail, RC, *Crusading Warfare* (Cambridge, 1956)

# Notes

**1: A New Hero**

i       Michael Attaleiates, *The History*, translated by Anthony Kaldellis and Dimitris Krallis (Dumbarton Oaks, 2012), p.181.

ii      Ibid., p.171.

iii     Ibid., p.181.

iv      Ibid., p.181.

**2: The Crisis of Byzantium**

v       Fulcher of Chartres, *A History of the Expedition to Jerusalem* (translated by Frances Rita Ryan) (University of Tennessee Press, 1973)

vi      Alan Harvey, *Economic Expansion in the Byzantine Empire 900–1200*; Angeliki E Laiou and Cécile Morrisson, *The Byzantine Economy.*

vii     Eric McGeer, 'Praecepta Militaria of Nikephorus Phocas' in *Sowing the Dragon's Teeth: Byzantine Warfare in the Tenth Century* (Dumbarton Oaks, 1995)

viii    Ibid, 'Al-Mutanabbi' quoted p.214.

ix      Leo the Deacon, *Leonis Diaconi Caloensis Historiae Libri Decem* (Bonn 1836) pp.50–51.

**3: Barbarians at the Gates**

x       Anna Comnena, *The Alexiad* (translated by ERA Sewter) (Penguin, 1969) p. 480.

## 4: The First Seljuk Attacks on Byzantium

xi      Michael Attaleiates, *The History*, translated by Anthony
        Kaldellis and Dimitris Krallis (Dumbarton Oaks, 2012), p.83.

xii     Matthew of Edessa, pp.111–13.

xiii    *Rashid al-Din*, translated by Luther, p.47.

xiv     Michael Attaleiates, *The History*, translated by Anthony
        Kaldellis and Dimitris Krallis (Dumbarton Oaks, 2012), p.147.

xv      Ibid., p.149.

xvi     Ibid., p.171.

## 5: The Last Roman Army

xvii    Michael Attaleiates, *The History*, translated by Anthony
        Kaldellis and Dimitris Krallis (Dumbarton Oaks, 2012), p.189.

xviii   Ibid., p.315.

xix     Ibid., p.191.

xx      Eric McGeer, *Sowing the Dragon's Teeth: Byzantine Warfare in the
        Tenth Century*, p.206.

xxi     Warren Treadgold, *Byzantium and Its Army 284–1081*.

## 6: The Syrian Campaign

xxii    Michael Attaleiates, *The History*, translated by Anthony
        Kaldellis and Dimitris Krallis (Dumbarton Oaks, 2012), p.209.

xxiii   Ibid., p.219.

xxiv    Ibid., p.219.

xxv     Ibid., p.221.

## 7: Normans and Turks

xxvi    Michael Attaleiates, *The History*, translated by Anthony
        Kaldellis and Dimitris Krallis (Dumbarton Oaks, 2012), p.231.

xxvii   Ibid., p.231.

xxviii  Ibid., p.233.

xxix    Ibid., pp.235–41.

xxx     Ibid., p.241.

## 8: War and Peace

xxxi    Michael Attaleiates, *The History*, translated by Anthony

Kaldellis and Dimitris Krallis (Dumbarton Oaks, 2012), p.253.

xxxii    Michael Psellus, *The Chronographia*, translated by E R A Sewter as *Fourteen Byzantine Rulers* (Penguin, 1966), p.354.

xxxiii    John Skylitzes, *A Synopsis of Byzantine History, 811–1057*, translated into English up to 1057 by John Wortley (Cambridge University Press, 2010). The period up to 1078 has not yet been translated.

xxxiv    Claude Cahen, 'La Campagne de Manzikert d'apres des sources Musselmanes', published in *Byzantion* Vol. 9, 1934, pp.613–42.

xxxv    Michael Attaleiates, *The History*, translated by Anthony Kaldellis and Dimitris Krallis (Dumbarton Oaks, 2012), p.255.

xxxvi    A C S Peacock, *The Great Seljuk Empire*.

xxxvii    Michael Attaleiates, *The History*, translated by Anthony Kaldellis and Dimitris Krallis (Dumbarton Oaks, 2012), p.259.

xxxviii    Ibid., p.257.

xxxix    Ibid., p.257.

## 9: The Road to Manzikert

xl    A C S Peacock, *Early Seljuk History* (Routledge 2010)

xli    Ibid., p.269.

xlii    Claude Cahen, 'La Campagne de Manzikert d'après des sources Musselmanes', published in *Byzantion* Vol. 9, 1934, pp.613–42.

## 10: The Armies Clash

xliii    *Nicephorus Bryennius, Historia*, translated by P Gautier.

xliv    Michael Psellus, *The Chronographia*, translated by E R A Sewter as *Fourteen Byzantine Rulers* (Penguin, 1966), p.354.

xlv    John Haldon, *The Byzantine Wars* (Tempus, 2001), p.117.

xlvi    Michael Attaleiates, *The History*, translated by Anthony Kaldellis and Dimitris Krallis (Dumbarton Oaks, 2012), p.273.

xlvii    Ibid., p.275.

xlviii    Ibid, p.271.

xlix    Ibid., p.277.

l    Ibid., p.277.

li    Ibid., p.279.

lii    Ibid., p.285.

liii      Ibid., p.289.

liv      Carole Hildenbrand, Translation of Nicephorus Bryennius in *Turkish Myth and Muslim Symbol: The Battle of Manzikert*, p245 (Edinburgh 2007)

**11: The Battle of Manzikert**

lv      Michael Attaleiates, *The History*, translated by Anthony Kaldellis and Dimitris Krallis (Dumbarton Oaks, 2012), p.291.

lvi      Ibid., p.291.

lvii      Ibid., p.293.

lviii      Carole Hillenbrand, Ibn al-Jawzi, as quoted in *Turkish Myth and Muslim Symbol: The Battle of Manzikert* (Edinburgh 2007).

lix      Ibid., p.293.

lx      Nicephorus Bryennius, *Historia*, translated by P Gautier.

lxi      Michael Attaleiates, *The History*, translated by Anthony Kaldellis and Dimitris Krallis (Dumbarton Oaks, 2012), p.293.

lxii      Ibid., p.293.

lxiii      Ibid., p.297.

lxiv      Ibid., p.295.

lxv      Carole Hillenbrand, *Turkish Myth and Muslim Symbol: The Battle of Manzikert*, quote from the account of al-Hussayni, p.56.

**12: Civil War**

lxvi      Michael Psellus, *The Chronographia*, translated by E R A Sewter as *Fourteen Byzantine Rulers*, (Penguin, 1966), p.357.

lxvii      Carole Hillenbrand, Text from al-Bundari, quoted in *Turkish Myth and Muslim Symbol: The Battle of Manzikert*, (Edinburgh 2007), p.263.

lxviii      Ibid., p.301.

lxix      Sibt Ibn al-Jawazi.

lxx      Michael Attaleiates, *The History*, translated by Anthony Kaldellis and Dimitris Krallis (Dumbarton Oaks, 2012), p.301.

lxxi      Ibid., p.303.

lxxii      Michael Psellus, *The Chronographia*, translated by E R A Sewter as *Fourteen Byzantine Rulers*, (Penguin, 1966), p.358.

lxxiii    Ibid., p.359.

lxxiv    Michael Attaleiates, *The History*, translated by Anthony
         Kaldellis and Dimitris Krallis (Dumbarton Oaks, 2012), p.315.

lxxv     Ibid., p.309.

lxxvi    Ibid., p.309.

lxxvii   Ibid., p.311.

lxxviii  Ibid., p.311.

lxxix    Ibid., p.317.

lxxx     Ibid, p.317.

lxxxi    Ibid., p.317.

lxxxii   Ibid., p.323.

lxxxiii  Ibid., p.325.

lxxxiv   Ibid., p.321.

## 13: The Collapse of Byzantium

lxxxv    John Skylitzes, *Brevarium Historicum*, Corpus Scriptorum
         Historiae Byzantinae, Bonn.

lxxxvi   Matthew of Edessa, *Chronicles*, translated into French by
         Eduard Dularier, Paris, 1858.

lxxxvi   Michael Attaleiates, *The History*, translated by Anthony
         Kaldellis and Dimitris Krallis (Dumbarton Oaks, 2012), p.347.

## 14 : Reflections on the Reign of Romanus Diogenes

lxxxviii Dimitris Krallis, *Michael Attaleiates and the Politics of Imperial
         Decline in Eleventh-Century Byzantium*.

lxxxix   George T Dennis, ed. by Michael Psellus, *Orationes Panegyricae*
         – quoted from Dimitris Krallis, *Michael Attaleiates and the
         Politics of Imperial Decline in Eleventh-Century Byzantium*.

xc       Dimitris Krallis, *Orationes Panegyricae*, ed. by Dennis, Oration
         19, p.96.

xci      Dimitris Krallis, *Orationes Panegyricae*, ed. by Dennis, Oration
         21:15–21, p.96.

xcii     Michael Attaleiates, *The History*, translated by Anthony
         Kaldellis and Dimitris Krallis (Dumbarton Oaks, 2012), p.219.

xciii    Michael Psellus, *The Chronographia*, translated by E R A Sewter
         as *Fourteen Byzantine Rulers*, (Penguin, 1966), p.356.

xciv    Michael Attaleiates, *The History*, translated by Anthony Kaldellis and Dimitris Krallis (Dumbarton Oaks, 2012), p.297.

xcv    Ibid., p.303.

### 15: Alexius Comnenus and the Call to the West

xcvi    Comnena, Anna, *The Alexiad* (translated by ERA Sewter) (Penguin, 1969), p.85.

xcvii    Ibid., p.140.

xcviii    Ibid., p.258

xcix    Ibid., p.101.

c    Peter Frankopan, *The First Crusade: The Call from the East* (Vintage, 2013)

ci    *Gesta Francorum*, (edited by Rosalind Hill) (Oxford, 1962), p.14.

cii    Comnena, Anna, *The Alexiad* (translated by ERA Sewter) (Penguin 1969), p.248.

ciii    Gregory VII, *Register*, I.46, p.51.

### 16: The March of the Crusaders

civ    Robert the Monk, *Historia Iherosolimitana*, RHC Occ. III, pp.727–28.

cv    *Gesta Francorum*, (edited by Rosalind Hill) (Oxford, 1962), pp.4–5.

cvi    Fulcher of Chartres, *A History of the Expedition to Jerusalem* (translated by Frances Rita Ryan) (University of Tennessee Press, 1973) pp.176–77.

cvii    Raymond of Aguilers, *Le Liber de Raymond d'Aguilers*, (translated by JH and LL Hill) (Paris, 1969), pp. 42–43.

cviii    *Gesta Francorum*, (edited by Rosalind Hill) (Oxford, 1962), p.20.

cix    Albert of Aachen, History of the Journey to Jerusalem (translated by Susan B Edginton) (Routledge, 2016)

cx    *Gesta Francorum*, (edited by Rosalind Hill) (Oxford, 1962), pp.19–21.

cxi    Ibid, p.21.

## 17: The Siege of Antioch

cxii     Fulcher of Chartres, *A History of the Expedition to Jerusalem* (translated by Frances Rita Ryan) (University of Tennessee Press, 1973)

cxiii    *Gesta Francorum*, (edited by Rosalind Hill) (Oxford, 1962)

cxiv    Fulcher of Chartres *A History of the Expedition to Jerusalem* (translated by Frances Rita Ryan) (University of Tennessee Press, 1973)

## 18: The Road to Jerusalem

cxv     Peter Frankopan, *The First Crusade: The Call from the East*, (Vintage, 2013), p.159.

cxvi    Raymond of Aguilers, *Le Liber de Raymond d'Aguilers*, (translated by JH and LL Hill) (Paris, 1969)

## 19: The Final Enemy

cxvii    Peter Tudebode, *Historia de Hieroslymitano itinere*, (translated JH and LL Hill) (Paris, 1977)

## Conclusion: The Stream of Time

cxviii   Comnena, Anna, *The Alexiad* (translated by ERA Sewter) (Penguin, 1969), p.17.

# INDEX

Page numbers in *italics* refer to maps

**Nick Holmes** studied history at Cambridge, where he was awarded a travel grant to follow the route of the First Crusade across Greece and Turkey. He has written a fictional novel, set in eleventh-century Byzantium, called *Trebizond*. He works in international finance and lives in Surrey with his family.